Endorsements for
RAZING HELL

I am thankful that Russ and Mave Moyer have the understanding that Deliverance is for today and they are not afraid to speak out the truth of God's Word. They recognize that Jesus gave the mandate to all Christians in Mark 16 to take authority over evil spirits and drive them out. They see the need for deliverance among Christians in bondage as they travel all over the world and that people perish for lack of knowledge. They are helping to bring back into the Church this mandate by Jesus that has been pushed aside and dismissed by most evangelical Christian leaders. This book will open the readers eyes to many aspects of spiritual warfare and inner healing, that when acted upon, can help the readers to begin to have more freedom to be what God wants them to be.

Roger Miller
Trumpet of Gideon Ministries

I am thrilled to endorse Brother Russ Moyer's book on spiritual warfare. Brother Russ brings clarity to an often misunderstood subject. He gives encouragement to those who are new in the spiritual warfare arena, at the same time, strengthening those who have been on the front lines for a while. He simplifies the mysterious while equipping the Body of Christ to take her place as His warrior bride. You will definitely want to add this book to your library. Thank you Brother Russ for a worthwhile and needed book.

Barbara "Mama Hug" Stephens
Abundant Life Ministries

With, *"I will build my church and the gates of hell will not prevail against it" (Matt 16:18)*, Jesus reveals the strength, steadfastness and standard of ones who are born again. What a wonderful opportunity we have to demonstrate the ministry of Jesus to our generation and to continue His work. Jesus went about anointed by the Holy Spirit destroying the works of the devil; John's epistle tells us that this was the purpose of His manifestation. We live in a world that is a battlefield and the war is waging for the souls of men in the souls of men. God has given us leaders who are preparing His people to not only wage war but to see triumph in this spiritual combat. Dr. Russ Moyer is a blessing to our generation and his understanding of the war, the weapons and the strategies God has given us for victory are not just idle words but tested and proven as they given him many testimonies of victory. Like the Paton, MacArthur and Montgomery he is one sent to his generation to help lead the greatest army that ever lived to certain victory over the most horrible enemy man has ever had.

Glenn Garland
Glenn Garland Ministries

Prepare to be practically equipped as a warrior in the end time battle! Razing Hell lays a firm foundation for successful spiritual warfare. Dr. Russ Moyer does a wonderful job of pairing personal testimonies with solid biblical teachings. As you read these anointed pages you will be moved to self-examination and personal empowerment to do the work of ministry! I highly recommend this book.

Rev Joanna Adams, Deliverance Coordinator
Eagle Worldwide Ministries

I am so pleased the Holy Spirit has prompted Dr. Russ Moyer to write this book explaining and clarifying true Spiritual Warfare and the power of consecrated intercessory prayer. He also explains freedom by deliverance of evil unclean spirits when deliverance is ministered in the same manner as Christ set captives free. This book is sound scriptural teaching for those in both the pulpit and the pew. There have been so many changes in the body of Christ since I received my Saviour seventy-one years ago. I have observed a noticeable lack of teachings concerning the New Birth experience. These include: Who we are as new Creatures in Christ (2 Cor. 5:17), our spiritual position in heavenly places (Eph. 2:6), our being endued with power through Holy Spirit baptism (Acts 1:8), our authority and power in Christ (Luke 10:19), to pray I faith as Jesus did to move mountains, i.e., our problems (Mark 11:23) and to pray effectively and prophetically calling those things that be not as through they were (Rom. 4:17).

That is why this book can be so helpful to all who read and receive from its solid scriptural truths.

Lovell McGuire
Deliverance Minister

Razing Hell: Learning to Fight the Powers and Principalities of the Night
Copyright © 2012 by Dr. Russ Moyer
ALL RIGHTS RESERVED

Unless otherwise noted, all Scripture quotations are from the King James Version of the Bible.

This is an Eagle Worldwide Publication

ISBN 978-0-9738172-5-6

Printed in the United States of America
For Worldwide Distribution

Eagle Worldwide Enterprises
P.O. Box 39
Copetown, ON, L0R 1J0
Canada

Tel.: (905) 308-9991
Fax.: (905) 308-7798
E-mail: enterprises@eagleworldwide.com
URL: http://www.eagleworldwide.com

Cover design by Miguel Simon
Name of book by Pastor Mave Moyer, given by revelation of the Holy Spirit.

This book or parts thereof may not be reproduced in any form without prior written permission from Eagle Worldwide Enterprises.

DEDICATION

I want to dedicate this book to a wonderful couple that have been a tremendous blessing to Mave and I. Thank you to Roger and Donna Miller of Franklin, TN. You both have been there with me from that turning point in my spiritual journey where I embraced the call to war. Your research, knowledge, training, information, input and personal ministry to Mave and I and all of Eagle Worldwide Ministries has been instrumental in developing us as an end time Healing and Resource Center. You have been wonderful and faithful partners and friends. Thank you.

ACKNOWLEDGEMENTS

This manual had been written, as a result of encouragement by other people, to provide material to prepare individuals to do Spiritual Warfare, and is part of a series that includes other practical manuals on intercessory prayer, deliverance and inner healing. After having received a number of prophetic words and confirmations concerning multiplication, duplication and reproduction, I have come to realize that the Lord has ordained this time as a time to impart, empower, enable and equip labourers for the end time harvest.

I am grateful to the Lord for having placed some individuals in my life to strengthen and encourage me and to sow in my life a walking, working, practical knowledge of Christian living. I am especially grateful to Pastor Paul Wetzel of Courts of Praise Fellowship in Pensacola Florida, who not only provided me with encouragement and counsel, but also opened up his heart and his Church, to provide me with a platform to work and flow freely in the gifts of the Spirit in these areas of ministry that are not only controversial, but have a tendency to generate persecution from within the Christian community.

I would also like to acknowledge the Eagle Worldwide leadership staff and team and especially Miguel Simon who helped so much with the cover design formatting and editing. Nellie Balandowich for compiling, editing and all clerical duties. All of you are such a blessing and encouragement to me. Thank you for your faithfulness.

I wouldn't be able to do much of what I do without the wonderful wife, helpmate, partner and friend the Lord has blessed me with. Mave, thank you for everything; the little and the large. When I found you I truly found a Good Thing.

TABLE OF CONTENTS

Foreword by Dr. Bill Sudduth .... *xi*

Introduction .... *xiii*

1. Role of the Apostolic in Warfare 15

2. Walking and Living in Alignment 25

3. The Mandate of Jesus and the Believer 45

4. Spiritual Warfare.. 51

5. Inner Healing 61

6. Sin, Curses and Unforgiveness 65

7. Prayer and Intercession.. 75

8. End Time Spirits 105

9. Testimonies 121

10. In Conclusion... 127

Bibliography

FOREWORD

I have known Russ Moyer as a friend and co-laborer since our days together in Bible School in the 1990's in Pensacola, Florida. Russ has always distinguished himself as a man who truly delights in the Lord. He displays a true hunger for the things of God in his life and in others. I've always known him as a true servant, always being a blessing, and always displaying the highest level of integrity.

Of all the folks I know that graduated from the Brownsville Revival School of Ministry. I don't know of anyone who has done more to advance the kingdom of God than Brother Russ. He has planting numerous churches in Canada. He has raised up and sent out anointed and gifted young men and women of God. He travels nationally and internationally. He is a planter and a builder, a true 21st century apostle who has written an outstanding book that reveals timeless truths in a fresh and relevant way.

This is not just another great book, and it's not just a book for folks involved in the deliverance ministry. It's a clarion call back to true holiness, and radical living, free of all bondages in our lives. It is a must read for all believers! I was truly blessed by reading it!

I encourage you to take the short time required to read it and to pray the prayers strategically placed in it. Here is your opportunity to be refreshed and revived, don't miss it.

Blessings,

Dr. Bill Sudduth
President
International Society of Deliverance Ministers
Colorado Springs, Colorado
USA

INTRODUCTION

It seems as though there is a tremendous amount of interest in this hour in the area of Spiritual Warfare and a renewed interest in the areas of deliverance, intercessory prayer and prophetic ministries. All of these areas of ministry interconnect and, to me, represent the end time ministries. There is no doubt in my mind that Jesus is coming back and that His return could be very soon. The harvest has already begun. I see it everywhere I go. I see the signs and wonders and miracles. I see lives dramatically changed and transformed, by the power of God.

"Razing Hell" was birthed a spiritual work in the heart of God. He birthed the title and sub-title in revelations to my wife, Mave. 'Razing' means: to tear down; demolish; level to the ground: to raze a row of old buildings. It also means to shave or scrape off.

In 1 John 3:8 the Bible says, *For this purpose the Son of God was manifested, that He might destroy the works of the devil.* Destroy is a synonym of raze (to reduce [an object] to useless fragments, a useless form, or remains, as by rending, burning, or dissolving; injure beyond repair or renewal; demolish; ruin; annihilate).

In Acts 10:38 we see that Jesus was anointed by God to heal all who were oppressed of the devil. According to Isaiah 10:27, the purpose of the anointing is to destroy the yoke, the yoke of the enemy. Not just break the yoke, but to destroy it, to annihilate it, to raze it and scrape it clean from the life of the believer.

I believe we need to focus on raising up radical, spirit filled labourers who are knowledgeable, anointed, and willing to do whatever is necessary to overcome — not just for themselves but also for others. That's right, to raise up.

Radical end-time warriors who have a burning desire in their hearts to 'raze' hell.

This it the time to raze hell, to totally destroy. It's time for this generation to receive that anointing. It's a time for kings and priests to go to war. Some prophets arc crying, "peace, peace!" but it's time to go to war. For it is the violent who take if by force (Matthew 11:12).

<u>ARISE</u> Church! This is our hour! Isaiah 60:1-2 says, "Arise, shine; for your light has come, and the glory of the Lord is risen upon thee. For, behold, the darkness shall cover the earth, and gross darkness the people: but the LORD shall arise upon thee, and his glory shall be seen upon thee."

In this, my first book on Spiritual Warfare, we will discuss the personal walk of an individual preparing for battle. How could we possibly move into the high levels of Spiritual Warfare such as intercession, deliverance and inner healing if our own personal walk and life are not in order? The Word of God says, **"Judge yourself that you would not be judged."**

This book is not meant to be a theological work but rather a practical guide that is easy to understand and implement in our daily lives. It is absolutely essential that we set a solid foundation to build on so that as we take the land in the name of the Lord we will be able to defend it. I believe this manual will help you to more effectively fulfill the call of God on your life, regardless of what area of ministry you are called to.

CHAPTER 1

ROLE OF THE APOSTOLIC IN WARFARE

As you are probably aware there is a great shift that has occurred in the body of Christ that actually began in 1948 when Israel prophetically stepped back into the land. A powerful prophetic parallel awakening has been occurring.

As Israel was being restored as a nation, as was its government, currency, language and culture, so has the church of Jesus Christ been experiencing a tremendous restoration back to the New Testament blueprint and model including the restoration of foundational truths such as five fold ministry, the cross, the blood and the power of His name. Kingdom precepts and principles have been replacing the administrative model of the church. The restoration of the Tabernacle of David according to Acts 15:16 *"After these things I will return, and I will rebuild the tabernacle of David which has fallen, and I will rebuild its ruins, and I will restore it,"* and certainly a focus on marketplace ministry. A church without walls, a church without boundaries.

A victorious church coming out in power and having a legitimate impact on the spheres of our society such as business, government, education and media. A church that's ready to rise up and take the land.

At the heart of this restoration is the birthing, building and development of the apostolic ministry and movement in the body of Christ. It is a calling forth of end time warriors and hand-maidens prepared and ready for battle, equipped and empowered; a prophetic generation. We are headed into a season of body ministry. No names, no faces, no agenda, but the agenda of God to extend and advance His Kingdom.

Whether we like it or not the battle lines have been established. There is a war going on. A war between good and evil, the plumb line has dropped and is dropping continually and that is from Amos 7:8. The hearts of men and nations are being tried and tested. There is an end time spiritual alignment that is taking place right now all over the earth.

Not just nations but in every home and family, in every church, in every city, in the lives of men and women everywhere the plumb line is dropping. There is a shaking that it going on prophetically in this hour. Everything that can be shaken will be shaken. That which remains that is rooted in the Word by the power of the Spirit will be the end time army that comes out without spot or without wrinkle. The bride that He is beckoning shall have the heart of David. Quick to go to a place of worship and intimacy, into the throne room of the almighty that was prepared through the blood of Jesus Christ, but also quick to go to battle.

As it was in the days of Nehemiah so it is today. This restoration includes the rebuilding of the spiritual walls of the church. Those called to action must have a weapon in one hand and a tool in the other. Like Joel's army, they will climb the walls like mighty men and not break rank. Having a true understanding of who they are in Christ and who Christ is in them.

This new spiritual alignment will be on a personal basis, a corporate basis and a Kingdom basis, alignments in our homes and in our churches. The Word of God says in Hosea 4:6 *"That for a lack of knowledge my people are destroyed."* Nowhere else is that more relevant than in the ministries related to spiritual warfare, such as deliverance, intercession and inner healing.

Prophetically, we stand now at the threshold of the greatest harvest ever known to man and also at the threshold of the greatest battle ever known to man.

As this harvest begins to come forth, it is not going to come without a fight. Jesus said that the violent shall take it by force — Matthew 11:12 *"From the days of John the Baptist until now the kingdom of heaven has suffered violence, and the violent take it by force."*

Many will come into the Kingdom of God from the highways and byways snatched by the love and Spirit of God from the jaws of the enemy. Those suffering from life altering addictions, rejection and heart ache, having fallen through cracks of our society; burdened physically, mentally and emotionally. They are going to need ministry. Not a fancy, pretty little prayer but a prayer full of power, not a long-winded religious prayer like the Pharisees of old prayed, but a prayer full of power and authority.

If you are reading this book, it is probably because you know somewhere down deep in your heart that God has called you and ordained you for battle. This book is not meant to be a theological work, but much more a practical work.

We are going to talk about how to come into alignment, how to do intercession and deliverance, because He wants to teach our hands to war.

HE TEACHETH MY HANDS TO WAR

In Psalm 18:34, David said, *"He teacheth my hands to war, so that a bow of steel is broken by mine arms."* I believe that in this hour the Lord is truly trying to teach His people to fight, and to fight the great spiritual battle that has already begun. Many times I have found that the Church avoids teaching on Spiritual Warfare, because they have already made a choice not to fight in the spiritual realm. For a long time we have almost completely avoided talking of demonic activity and it's influence on the members of the Church, born again Christians.

Whether we choose to fight or not fight, that doesn't mean that the enemy won't fight. The battle began long ago and Jesus shined the light of revelation on the purposes of Satan, which is to steal, kill and destroy, and the target is the same now as it was then. It is not the land, but mankind that he attacks. If we don't fight are we still a target? Certainly!

There is no indication in the Word that Adam and Eve ever attacked the devil, yet he plotted to separate them from God. By us ignoring him, and even at times saying he doesn't exist, we play right into his scheming hand. Paul tells us in Ephesians 6:12, exactly who the enemy is, and where the battle lies. *"For we wrestle not against flesh and blood, but against principalities, powers against the rulers of the darkness of this world, against spiritual wickedness in high places."* The Word clearly identifies the enemy.

Our battle is not with one another. Every time we try to fight in the natural realm, bringing conflict, strife and disunity to the body, we rob ourselves of the blessing. He certainly does not want us to be ignorant concerning how to do battle, because the Word says in Hosea 4:6 *"The people are destroyed for a lack of knowledge."* I am going to discuss in this manual and outline here in the first chapter some very simple and fundamental principles and techniques of Spiritual Warfare.

When a soldier is called to war, particularly in North America, his training is three-fold, and I believe that is the same concept the Lord would use to prepare His soldiers for Spiritual Warfare. First, basic training, second, advanced training and third, specialized training. The basic training is training on the fundamentals and foundations of being a soldier, and no matter what your function is in the army, everyone needs to learn the fundamentals of being a soldier. Things like having a disciplined daily walk. We all need to be grounded in the Word, men and women of prayer and prepared to worship Him in Spirit and in truth.

In advanced training, we need to get an understanding of spiritual authority, as who I am in Christ and who Christ is in me, and the spiritual authority that has been given to me. We also need to understand important principles of Spiritual Warfare such as spiritual alignment on a personal and family basis as well as in the Church and the spiritual covering that the Lord has placed us in submission to, for our own protection. And of course, consecration which sounds like a big word, but simply means: I surrender all. It is about putting first things first, like the first of the Ten Commandments. In Exodus 20:3 says, *"thou shalt have no other gods before me."*

I believe consecration must be done in three areas: your material possessions, your relationships and of course consecration of yourself — your hopes, goals and dreams. I will discuss more about this in chapter two on consecration. Also in the advanced training, we start directly addressing the issues of holiness. Holiness is essential, for every soldier in the army of God. It empowers our walk; it enhances our relationship with Christ and strengthens our prayer. When we go to meet with God, it clearly states in Psalm 24 that those who desire to mount the hill of God need to do so with clean hands and a pure heart. Holiness is part of the preparation of meeting God. The Word says that those who know their God will do great and might exploits. It is out of relationship that the power of God, signs and wonders are released to us and through us. Holiness insures us of a powerful prayer life, because the Word says that the prayers of a righteous man availeth much!

Finally, He moves us on to specialized training, where we receive the assignment as to what Church/ministry we are to be affiliated with and we begin to walk in the Spirit, walking in areas of Christian relationship and accountability in fellowship with other believers, who may be similarly called to a particular style of ministry and/or assigned to a certain Church, area or region. In my opinion a Christian walk is not to be walked alone. I believe to truly be in fellowship, we must walk as Paul walked, under proper spiritual authority and covering, (Peter and the council of elders) and we must walk hand in hand with our peers in a team concept of ministry as Paul did with Barnabas and Silas. As we walk in that place of ideal relationship and accountability, we must also have our Timothy. I believe discipleship and mentorship is an important part of what God is doing in this hour to strengthen His Church. It is usually in the specialized training where we really begin to get a stronger awareness of the weapons of warfare.

THE WEAPONS OF WARFARE

1. Praise and worship are both offensive and defensive weapons. It tells us in Psalm 8:2 that the Lord ordained praise to silence the voice of the enemy. We also know that through praise and worship we enter into the glory, which pushes back all darkness, as we stand in the presence of God.

2. Binding and loosing, in Matthew 16:19, the Lord said *"And I shall give unto you the keys to the kingdom and whatsoever you shall bind on earth shall be bound in heaven, and whatsoever you shall loose on earth shall be loosed in heaven."* We need to believe that promise and begin to bind the influences that are attacking us, our families, our churches, and our nations, and begin to loose the blessing of God over those situations, and speaking and releasing the fruit of the Spirit.

3. We need to begin to exercise our faith. Without faith it is impossible to please God. Everything we receive in the Spiritual realm, we receive by faith. We need to stop giving lip service to the word 'faith.' Just saying we believe is not enough. In James 2:17 it says that *"faith if it has not works is dead."* We need to tap into that mountain moving faith as Jesus spoke of in Mark 11:22-25, where He stated, have faith in God and through that faith God will move mountains. Man cannot move mountains nor can man move God. Faith moves God! He marveled at the faith of the centurion and honoured that faith and confirmed it with the miracle. Let's activate our faith, in God, so that He can move the mountains out of our way.

Recently my daughter Melissa re-taught and demonstrated to me a great life lesson. Never under-estimate the power of a mother's prayers, love or faith. My grandson was unconscious for five days in a coma and on life-support. Melissa spoke life, hope, healing and love over him. She would now allow the doctors, nurses or visitors speak any negative words in his presence or in the hospital room. He miraculously regained consciousness and is on the road to a full recovery. We prayed, laid hands on James, anointed him with oil, made bold declarations and proclamations over him, fought the battle and waged war for him when he was not able to fight for himself.

4. We need to get a hold of His power weapons. There is power in the blood. There is power in His name, the power of His love and, if there is any power at all, there is the power of prayer. We need to begin to activate the power weapons in the Church. We need to begin to teach on the power that we have in Christ: how, when and where we appropriate this power, where it operates best and what we are to use it for. Without that knowledge, we are destroyed, defeated in battle.

5. We need to begin to acknowledge that the Spiritual gifts are for now. The five fold ministry is for now, as outlined in Ephesians 4:11-12, so that we can receive the blessing that was intended for us by Christ when He gave His Church these five ministry office gifts. Every minister is not called to be a Pastor or an Evangelist. Each of these gifting areas has some specific role, function and blessing that need to be released and received by the Church. We need to acknowledge the gifting area so that we can receive the intended blessing. From the Pastor: the shepherding, direction and love. From the Teacher: the knowledge, training and revelation of the Word. From the Evangelist: the powerful heart and burden to reach the world with the message of the gospel. The Prophet: from him the revelation, the guidance, the direction of where we are headed next as he sounds the trumpet to prepare us for battle.

In 2 Chronicles 20:20 he instructs us that if you *"believe in the Lord your God, so shall you be established and believe his prophets and so shall you prosper."* Let us not hinder the prosperity and blessing of the Lord with our unbelief. The Apostles of this hour will carry the great blessings of the Apostles of old: the wisdom of God. They will plant churches, pastor pastors, walk in signs and wonders, and if we will acknowledge them and receive them, it will enable us to hold the great harvest that is on the way. The purpose of the five fold (according to Ephesians 4:12) is to perfect the saints for the work of ministry for the edifying of the body of Christ The five fold needs to equip, empower and release warriors into the harvest.

6. We need a fresh stirring of the nine signature gifts of the Holy Spirit as described by Paul in 1 Corinthians 12:1. We also need to recognize that all of these are for today! Word of knowledge, word of wisdom, the gift of faith, gifts of healing, working of miracles, gift of prophecy, discerning of spirits, tongues and interpretation of tongues. Paul instructs us in chapter 12 verse 1, *"Now concerning spiritual gifts brethren I would not have you ignorant."* Again, the Lord wants us to be knowledgeable, not ignorant of the weapons of warfare, to insure our victory.

7. The Word. There is power in the written word, the logos. The Word of God is the sword of the Spirit. We need to use it on the enemy. We need the rhema word the word of revelation, for each of us. These are the days of revelation glory. Man does not live by bread alone but by every word spoken from the mouth of God. The Word that gives us the stops and the goes, the rights and the lefts. Finally, we need the prophetic word. We need to use the prophetic word to make bold proclamations, and to call things into being that are not: to pray as though it were. When someone speaks a prophetic word to us, we need to heed and honour the word of instruction that Paul gave to Timothy, in 1 Timothy 1:18-19. To commit ourselves to the prophecies that were given us, to fight the good warfare, and hold the faith in good conscience, so that we do not find ourselves shipwrecked.

The apostle Paul exhorted us in 1 Corinthians 14:1 right after a great teaching on the gifts of the Spirit and the gift of love to, *Pursue love, yet desire earnestly spiritual gifts, but especially that you may prophesy* (NASB).

8. As we prepare for battle daily we need to honestly put on the armour of God. We all talk about it, but unfortunately I find that many people, don't really utilize this great defensive weapon that Paul described so aptly in Ephesians 6:11-19 — both their application and their function.

I close this opening chapter, by dispelling one of the half-truths that we seem to continue to spread in spiritual and Church circles: that God is loving, kind, peaceful, full of mercy and grace. He is all of that, but He is much, much more. He is the God of righteousness, holiness and judgment. He is a mighty warrior. The Word tells us in Exodus 15:30, *The Lord is a man of war: the Lord is his name.* That's right, the Lord is a man of war!

THE LORD IS A MAN OF WAR! THE LORD IS HIS NAME! Hallelujah!

CHAPTER 2

WALKING AND LIVING IN ALIGNMENT
A DAILY WALK

In this chapter, I'm going to outline for you a typical daily walk of a Christian. Keep in mind however, that the walk of a Christian is anything but typical or normal. The One we follow was a radical revolutionary who turned the world upside down nearly 2000 years ago. Even as we speak, people throughout the world are coming to the knowledge of our Lord and Saviour, Jesus Christ, and walking to the beat of a different drummer.

In my opinion, the walk of a Christian should be a walk of dedication, revelation, relationship and determination. We need to dedicate ourselves to the will, plan and purpose of God for our lives. We need to dedicate ourselves to come to know Him better, and the only way to do that is for us to take the initiative and time necessary to nurture a relationship.

Every man or woman who ministers in the Spirit will do so out of that place of relationship. The Word of God says in Daniel 11:32 *"Those who know their God will do, great and mighty exploits."* We therefore, must be dedicated to seek Him in the Word and in prayer, in a form of devotion but not ritual. Each day we need to spend time reading and studying God's Word so that we can allow His Word to renew our minds.

At the time we accept Jesus as Lord and Saviour, the Lord possesses our spirit. Our spirit is His immediately, paid for with a price, the blood of Jesus Christ. However, our mind, will and emotions — which comprise our soul — must be renewed by the daily washing of the water of the Word. Prayer is very essential as well. To me, prayer is fellowship and a one-on-one communion with God. It is in that place of fellowship, that Paul maintained that he prayed without ceasing.

Certainly each of us should and ***must*** pray 'without ceasing.' Nevertheless, I also believe that we need to set aside specific times of devotion where we can take ourselves away from the hustle and bustle of daily life and get into the Glory of the Lord. How do we get into the Glory? It's so simple!

One of the most wonderful opportunities of my life was when the Lord allowed me to serve with Sister Ruth Heflin at Calvary Pentecostal Tabernacle in Ashland, Virginia. Sister Ruth was a prophetess to the Nations, and her ministry focused on worship. We do warfare through worship. Her ministry was noted for its prophetic anointing and revelation and her ability to lead people into the Glory realm through spontaneous worship. Her formula was ever so simple: praise until the Spirit of worship comes and then worship till the Glory comes, then stand in the Glory.

The Glory is the manifest presence of God. There is the Omni-presence where God is everywhere, but there is the manifest presence of God, where you can feel, taste and sense His wonderful presence. This is the Glory realm. It is in that place where revelation is birthed; where we can hear the voice of the Lord, His prompting, guidance, direction and His love, are all in the Glory realm. All that we need is in the Glory realm. All things are possible in the Glory realm — hearts are mended and lives are changed.

When you first begin to go to that place of relationship and prayer, you must expect opposition and, like anything else, the more you practice, the better you get and the easier it becomes. This will lead you to walk in that place of fellowship as Paul did, as Sister Ruth did, and as many other men and women of God are doing today, where they pray and fellowship without ceasing. I mentioned that determination would highlight the Christian walk and it takes determination, even discipline, to breakthrough.

Initially, to take and set aside that time is the first form of opposition we encounter. Many times, doing good things, or even important things, even ministry, will sidetrack us. The enemy will try to keep us busy because he knows the person who cultivates that relationship and that daily communication in prayer is a threat to the kingdom of darkness. It's in that place of fellowship that warriors are born.

The next area of opposition that would come many times is through distractions. Start to pray, and the doorbell or phone will ring, dogs begin barking, kids will call for mom or some other mental distractions will come. Sometimes, it can seem like you're having a very peaceful, quiet day until you step into that place of fellowship and prayer and just try to quiet yourself before the Lord then . . . "OH BOY!" Look out! Everything on your 'To-Do List' — groceries, cleaning, school, the bills, begins flashing across your mind. **"BANG!"** That's the battleground.

Wasn't Calvary called the Place of the Skull? That's where the battle was waged. That's where it was waged then and now. Jesus won it for us then, but we also have a responsibility! We need to take control of our own minds. *Casting down imaginations, and every high thing that exalteth itself against the knowledge of God, and bringing into captivity every thought to the obedience of Christ* (2 Corinthians 10:5).

These are a few things in our daily walk that we really need to do:

1. Walk in fellowship with other Christians.

2. Walk separately from the world.

2 Cor. 6:17 *"Wherefore come out from among them and be ye separate, saith the Lord, and touch not the unclean thing; and I will receive you."*

Gal. 5:25, 26 *"If we live in the Spirit, let us also walk in the Spirit. Let us not be desirous of vain glory, provoking one another, envying one another."*

3. Walk in unity one with another. In that Spirit of unity there is a commanded blessing as found in Psalm 133:1 *"Behold, how good and how pleasant it is for brethren to dwell together in unity."* This is where there is a commanded blessing, when brothers dwell in unity.

WALKING IN ALIGNMENT

If we are going to be effective in the area of spiritual warfare, we are going to have to be men and women who understand spiritual authority and walk and live in alignment. Watchman Nee, in his book "Spiritual Authority" says, "A spiritual man is not a man just born again, but a man born again **walking in alignment**."

We see in Ephesians Chapter 2:18-22, *"[18] for through Him we both have our access in one Spirit to the Father. [19] So then you are no longer strangers and aliens, but you are fellow citizens with the saints, and are of God's household, [20] having been built on the foundation of the apostles and prophets, Christ Jesus Himself being the corner stone, [21] in whom the whole building, being fitted together, is growing into a holy temple in the Lord, [22] in whom you also are being built together into a dwelling of God in the Spirit."* The Holy Spirit is speaking through Paul about the supernatural alignment that is necessary in the church and about building a spiritual house, a dwelling place, and a holy habitation. He states that the church or the spiritual house is to be built on the foundation of apostles and prophets and that Jesus Christ Himself is the chief cornerstone.

Any of us who understand the construction of a building in the natural know the chief cornerstone is not the foundation. It is the first stone laid upon the foundation. Its purpose is alignment and every stone after that first stone is laid needs to come into alignment with the chief cornerstone. I submit to you that one of the primary purposes of

Christ in the building of the New Testament church is alignment. Every lively stone that Peter refers to in the building of the spiritual house in 1 Peter 2:4-7 must come into alignment with this chief cornerstone which is Christ. *"[4]And coming to Him as to a living stone which has been rejected by men, but is choice and precious in the sight of God, [5] you also, as living stones, are being built up as a spiritual house for a holy priesthood, to offer up spiritual sacrifices acceptable to God through Jesus Christ. [6] For this is contained in Scripture: "Behold, I lay in Zion a choice stone, a precious corner stone, and he who believes in him will not be disappointed. [7] This precious value, then, is for you who believe; but for those who disbelieve, the stone which the builders rejected, this became the very corner stone."*

He speaks of us as a holy priesthood, a chosen people, precious in the sight of God and lining up with the chief cornerstone, which is Christ. This alignment must take place in every area of our life, including church and family; consecrating all things to Him and Him alone.

CHURCH ALIGNMENT

In this hour I believe the Lord is calling His church to walk in a place of discipleship and mentorship. As it was in the beginning of the church, it is now. I believe that every Christian needs to emulate that place that Paul walked. He understood discipleship and mentorship — where He walked under authority to Peter and the other council of Apostles. He walked beside his brother in the faith and partner in ministry, Barnabas. Paul walked in that place of mentorship to Timothy and Titus. This is the hour before the 'Great and Terrible Day of the Lord' when He shall turn the hearts of the Fathers to the children . . . Malachi 4:5-6 *"Behold, I will send you Elijah the prophet before the coming of the great and dreadful day of the LORD: And he shall turn the heart of the fathers to the children, and the heart of the children to their fathers, lest I come and smite the earth with a curse."*

It's time we walk in that place of discipleship and mentoring where we are accountable to one another, not just to raise others up, but also to hold others up. It's time to be there for others, not only in their times of strength but also in their times of weakness, in their moments of joy and their moments of sadness. This way we can all share in the victory that Christ won and walk together in the harvest that He promised.

Before we consider launching out into areas of warfare, first and foremost we need to have the prayer covering. We all need the covering of a local church and everybody needs a pastor. That's right, **everybody** needs a pastor. A prophet needs a pastor, a teacher needs a pastor, an apostle needs one, even a pastor needs a pastor . . . and you and I need a pastor. I believe that this is the hour that we will see the restoration of the "five-fold ministry" and the realignment of the church and restoration of the apostolic order. I believe we are going to see the five-fold ministry in working order, according to Ephesians 4, cooperating together under the proper spiritual authority; and that covering and protection funneling down over the saints. I believe it's also the time when the church will begin to move into a place of body ministry where the Body of Christ will do the work of the ministry as it was designed to do.

I believe it is in this place of proper alignment that the church will fulfill its destiny. It will not be until we as believers settle into that place of alignment under the proper spiritual authority that we will be able to walk, live and operate in the fullness of the power that the Lord has for us.

We need more than just spiritual authority in the church for us to be in proper alignment. We need to have proper spiritual authority in our **homes**. Only when we walk in authority in our homes does our family have the full protection from the fiery darts of the enemy.

FAMILY ALIGNMENT

First and foremost, Christ needs to be the head of every family. If we're married — then the husband needs to align himself under the covering of Christ and every godly husband/father has a perfect role model. As Christ loves His children, each and every one of us, His love covers us with His protection; as does our natural father. Also, as Christ shows His love and protection through His relationship with His bride the church, then we as Godly husbands must emulate and supply that love and protection for our families. Whether we're married or single, we must put ourselves under the proper family alignment.

Wives, according to the Word of God, are to walk in a place of submission. In this day of individuality, individual rights, and in the light of past abuses both in the family and in the church, the word "submission" has taken on a very negative connotation. For a wife to walk in submission does not in any way mean that she is to be a doormat, or that she is not to share in family decisions, because the Lord views us as one. I believe that almost always if a husband and wife are walking in alignment and submission to Christ that they will walk in a place of agreement, power and authority. When there is disagreement, it certainly is a sign that something is <u>not</u> in order and should at least raise a caution flag. Such situations should cause us to take time and seek the Lord so that when we move, we will know we are walking acceptable to His perfect will. I feel it is not proper for a wife to take the place of authority in the home.

Sometimes women do this with their own personal motives according to their own personality or ambition, etc. At other times, they feel forced to do it because their husbands have not taken that place of headship in the home. Even at other times, men release their wives into this role because of laziness, lack of initiative, or fear, and abdicate that leadership role. In any case, this is the moment, this is the time for husbands and wives to correct the situation and get back into Godly family alignment (Ephesians 5).

I want you to know that my wonderful wife Mave and I do not agree on everything, but I love her, appreciate her and value and respect her opinion. When we disagree, one of us usually chooses to be in agreement and because we understand the power of unity and agreement, one of us will make the choice or agree to commit that issue to the Lord in further prayer.

Children must honour their parents, and for their own good, walk in proper alignment. In some cases, children choose, by their own free will, to disobey their parents or walk in rebellion. At these times, they move themselves out from under the protective covering and cut-off the flow of blessing that God has for them in their life.

Unfortunately today I observe families out of alignment in regard to the parent/child relationship and in many cases the children are running the home. This is not a healthy situation for either the parent or the child. The fault can be on either side. Many parents in my generation grew up in very strict and sometimes abusive family situations and vowed not to allow that to happen when they became parents or that they wanted to be friends with their children. I have to remember that my Godly role and ordained responsibility is to be my child's parent not their friend, and encourage them to make good friends and proper relationships.

When we're walking in that proper place of alignment, there are many benefits (Ephesians 6). Here are three of those benefits:

1. Spiritual covering and protection. Making it a safe environment for myself and all family members that creates an atmosphere of respect and honor conducive to learning and decision-making.

2. We are able to hear the voice of God more clearly and utilize the safe-guards the Lord put into play in the marriage relationship, since He views us as one. According to the Word of God, our prayers will not be hindered but rather more powerful and effective.

3. We allow ourselves to live in homes and family relationships that are more orderly and peaceful when each of us assumes the role that God earmarked for us in the family. We also are creating a model of family for future generations that our children may emulate and when viewed out of our community of faith, will be a good witness for the Lord.

INDIVIDUAL ALIGNMENT

Having just described proper alignment in the church and in the family, let's now move on to the final place that I feel spiritual authority is essential and that's in each individual. Man is a triune being — spirit, soul, and body. As I stated earlier, at the moment of rebirth, our spirit is possessed by God and changed.

Your soul needs to be renewed by the washing of the water of the Word and your body must come under submission to your spirit and soul. When you submit your spirit to Christ, it then comes into alignment with the Spirit of God. You must now consciously and clearly make a decision to place your soul (mind/will/emotions) in submission to your spirit. You must consciously and daily make a decision to put your body in proper alignment to your soul and spirit. As many of you know, your body has desires of its own. It must come into submission to your spirit and your soul. You are probably aware that your soul generates thoughts of its own. You must bring these thoughts under the authority of God and submit them to your spirit. Emotions can go up and down like a roller-coaster if you allow them. You must decide to bring them into proper alignment.

In the end, many of us want to make our own decisions, guide ourselves in our own direction and do things based on our own will. You must place your will, desires, thoughts, and emotions into proper alignment to your spirit. Sometimes the body even seems to have a mind of its own. If let go, without discipline and proper choices and submission to the soul and spirit, the body will be attacked and defiled by over and under indulgences in every area of your life. So, proper alignment is your body submitting to your soul, your soul submitting to your spirit, and your spirit surrendered and yielded to the Spirit of God. Paul called this "Crucifying the Flesh."

Take time to read the following verses from Ephesians 5:20-33 and 6:1-8. As you review them, you will see that much of this teaching comes directly from the Word of God. The Word of God tells us to put on the Mind of Christ.

CONSECRATION

Consecration can be simply defined or described as placing everything in our lives in the proper relationship with God. The only proper relationship between God and man is that we let nothing come between God and us; not material goods, not relationships, not out own desires.

Consecration means to set apart. When we commit ourselves to God, we set ourselves apart for His plan, His purpose and His use. The act of consecration is described ever so aptly in the hymn, "I surrender all."

I SURRENDER ALL

All to Jesus I surrender; all to him I freely give.
I will ever love and trust Him; in His presence daily live.
I surrender all, I surrender all
All to Him, my precious Saviour,
I surrender all.

Anytime that we allow things or people or plans that we have for our life to get out of proper perspective and put them between us and God, or we put them on the same level of importance as God, it's idolatry. We then, must reconsecrate ourselves to Him.

Webster's Dictionary defines an "idol" as a representative or symbol or an object of worship. An idol can be anything or anyone that we treasure, seek or care about more than God. It is idolatry when we place these things or people at the same or higher priority in our life than we do God. The first two commandments God gave to man through Moses in Exodus 20:3-4, clearly stated that we are to have no other Gods before Him, and that we would not make for ourselves an idol, in the form of anything in heaven above, or in the earth beneath or in the waters below.

When speaking to most people especially in North America, it seems as though one of the most common excuses I receive as to why men or women who express a great love of God are not seeking Him more diligently, is time. I have trouble accepting that as a viable excuse. After spending 21 years in business, at times with as many as 175 employees, when I needed to get things done and I wasn't able to do it myself, I normally looked for a busy person because I found they knew how to prioritize things in their life.

Secondly, I would observe people who never had time to perform important functions that had to do with their career or livelihood and in one breath would complain about no time to do anything, but you flash two tickets to a ball game or a hockey match in front of them and they would immediately find time. This tells me that almost always we have time for that which we care most about.

I found that to be true, not only in the area of time, which is a substance of our life that we only have a set amount of, but also in the area of resources or finances. If you want a good indication of the role and order of priority that God plays in your life, just open up your cheque book and see where you spend most of your money. The Lord says that where a man's heart is, his treasure is there also.

There are three main areas that we are going to focus on in consecration:

1. Material Possessions
2. Relationships
3. Self-Consecration

MATERIAL POSSESSIONS

Let's start with materialism. Having spent most of my life in North America, I have found materialism to be the largest obstacle and hindrance to Christianity. There seems to be an underlying and burning desire in people to accumulate things. In many cases it has been inbred from childhood to equate personal success with the accumulation of material goods. To many of those who worship at the altar of materialism, their motto is: the one who dies with the most toys wins! Obviously this quest for material possessions makes us vulnerable and opens doors for the enemy to attack us through financial pressure, job stress, and competitive spirits, like comparing ourselves with others and unworthiness.

The three biggest problems in my opinion are:

1. When we have an emotional need or problem in our life, instead of going to God to help us overcome this difficulty, we head to the shopping centre or we open the refrigerator or we engage in some escapism, such as a recreational activity.

2. We go to work to try to earn more money to purchase more goods to make us feel more worthy. Well, I've found that it works the opposite way and this type of thinking just feeds off of itself and tends to lead us in a vicious circle.

3. At the moment that we attempt to undertake a spiritual activity, such as prayer, Church attendance or Bible study, the enemy will find a way to use these things to distract us from our devotion and worship of God.

I want you to know that I am not opposed, nor do I feel God is opposed to our having material possessions. The Word of God does not say, that money is the root of all evil, but rather in 1 Timothy 6:10 the Bible clearly states, *"the love of money is the 'root' of all evil."* Therefore, the object of consecration of material possessions is to keep these things from becoming idols in our lives and distractions to our relationship with Christ. We must continually put these things under our feet, so that the enemy can't hold them over our head.

One final thought on materialism, when Jesus spoke to the rich young ruler in Luke 18:18-30, He said to His Disciples, that it was difficult, NOT impossible and one way that allows it to be possible is that we possess these things and they do not possess us. It's by keeping everything in the proper perspective and making the most important thing in our life, the most important thing. That's our relationship with Christ.

Let's take a moment now, and just place the things in our life figuratively under our feet, by surrendering everything in our life to Christ again. Let's put it on the altar and say to Him, if this object in possession is affecting my relationship with you, Lord Jesus, I surrender it to you! You can have it. You can take it. In Jesus' name. Amen.

RELATIONSHIPS

The second area of Consecration is relationships. Any one who reads the Word of God will realize that God places a high regard on family and other relationships.

In Ephesians, He clearly outlines how we are to inter-relate to one another within the family and in Matthew 22:37-39 Jesus gave us the two new commandments; *"Love the Lord your God with all your heart and with all your mind. This is the first and greatest commandment. And the second is like it: "Love your neighbour as yourself."* In these Scriptures, I believe He not only told us the importance of loving one another and of loving God, but He also gave us the proper order, God first then, others.

It's never clearer than in Matthew 10:37, *"Anyone who loves his father and mother more than me is not worthy of me; anyone who loves his son or daughter more than me is not worthy of me."* If we love anyone more or put that relationship before God, He considers us unworthy to be called His follower. Every relationship in our life must be consecrated to God, even family. When we begin to put our children or our spouse first, then they become an idol to us, and prevent us from making our relationship with Christ the #1 priority in our life.

Many of us, who have accepted the call of God on our life and work in either full or part-time ministry or serve as a Christian Worker, will realize that when we step out to serve the Lord, the enemy will attack someone we love or care about. If when this loved one comes under attack, we stop doing the Work of God we are called to do and go to the aid of that loved one; we will find that we allowed Satan to beat us twice. First the loved one, and then by distracting us from the work we're called to do. Once we fall for this tactic of the enemy, then every time we step out to the forefront, that moment of important service, the enemy, you and the Lord will all know that all he needs to do to stop us is to pull the cord on your loved one.

When dealing in the front lines, end time ministries such as intercession, deliverance, evangelism, and the prophetic, we can expect attacks as well as persecution. Like the disciples in the Book of Acts, we need to pray for holy boldness. We also need to make a commitment on a regular basis, to consecrate every relationship in our life, our parents, our spouse, our children, our peers, and our friends. We need to consecrate them, even unto death, even as Abraham did his son in Genesis 22.

At the same time the Lord wants us to live balanced lives honouring and loving family and friends. His heart is also to bless us in every way: financially, spiritually, in our families and in our careers. He is a blessing God and wants us to be successful in every area of our lives according to Joshua 1:8 *This book of the law shall not depart out of thy mouth; but thou shalt meditate therein day and night, that thou mayest observe to do according to all that is written therein: for then thou shalt make thy way prosperous, and then thou shalt have good success.*

Let's pray now, this prayer together — Father, I come to you in Jesus name and in the Power of the Holy Spirit and I lay these individuals upon your altar. I ask you to help me, not to allow these relationships to hinder or interfere in any way with my dedication and relationship with you. I place them on the altar today, trusting you and knowing that you are able to take care of all the needs of my loved ones. In Jesus' name. Amen.

SELF-CONSECRATION

This is probably the most difficult area of consecration for any one of us to step into. Probably the number one reason why Christ would not be on the throne of our life is because we're already occupying that seat. I don't think anyone of us could blame Him one bit for not wanting to share His Lordship with us. Is He really Lord of our life? He is either Lord of All, or He is not Lord at all. If our hopes and dreams and goals and plans come first, or if we have allowed sin; such as pride, rebellion, unforgiveness or selfishness to reign in our life, then He can't reign. Just saying He's Lord doesn't make it so. Our actions, our thoughts, words and deeds, speak loud and clear of the position He holds in our hearts and in our lives.

Don't get me wrong, I believe that the Lord wants us to set personal goals, to have plans and ambition, to look toward the future. I also believe that He wants us to live balanced lives that include some outside activities and personal pleasures, but first and foremost we must submit our will to His Will. We must also seek Him for guidance and direction in our lives and we must get the sin out of our life because sin separates us from God.

Again, we must leave no place for sin. Sin is the enemy of God. Disobedience and rebellion are sin. When we do not conform our will to His, or when we put our will and our plan before His, it's plain and simple rebellion and disobedience. That's sin. There's no better time than now for us to consecrate ourselves wholly and fully to God and to put these things under our feet.

Let's pray together — Heavenly Father, I ask you now, to have the Holy Spirit reveal to me any sin in my life and I repent for having allowed my plans, goals, ambitions or personal pleasure to come before or interfere with my relationship with you. I repent and I ask you to forgive me and help me now, as I consecrate these things of self to you. I choose to put them under my feet and walk not in the things of the flesh, but to be led and guided by your spirit. Help me as I rededicate myself to you. In Jesus' Name. Amen.

This is the time when we need to be certain that we have fully consecrated every aspect of our life to God, all possessions, relationships and self. We need every one of us to answer the question in 1 Chronicles 29:5(b) where David asked in prayer, *"and who then is willing to consecrate his service this day unto the Lord?"*

WALKING IN RELATIONSHIP

Proverbs 27:17 says, *"as iron sharpens iron, so one man sharpens another."* Am I my brother's keeper? Cain was the author of that question; he was not one of my bible heroes!

I believe that we as Christians are to walk in fellowship, relationship and peace whenever possible with one another.

I believe that one of the most important ingredients missing in the present day Church of Jesus Christ is in the area of mentorship/discipleship. We need to walk in a place of openness, transparency and accountability.

I believe that the day of the lone ranger, walking and even ministering by himself, shooting from the hip, is gone. It has cost the Church more than it was worth.

I believe we are walking in the day and in the hour of team ministry so that the Church can give the glory and honour and praise, not to a man but to the Lord.

I don't think it was by coincidence that in Luke 10, when He sent out the seventy into the harvest, He sent them out two by two, to walk together in unity, to protect one another, to hold one another up and to be accountable one to another. When we walk, two or more together and there is a burden, trial or tribulation, it is only half as heavy and when we share the victory, it is twice as good! I find that almost every where I go, that people are beginning to form small groups, cells, fellowships and teams, some based on gender, some based on common gifts, callings and purposes of ministry, others having to do with geographical location.

These small groups are an ideal setting to develop deeper inter-personal relationships and minister to one another. It is a place where we can be open and transparent and address real life issues that we are facing and doing battle on a daily basis.

To give you an example, men's groups can openly address the issues facing men, such as lust, pornography, masturbation, and other real life issues like the difference between being the priest of our home and the dictator, and can a real man cry? It is time to face the fact that the sins of the fathers go to the third and the fourth generation (*The LORD is longsuffering, and of great mercy, forgiving iniquity and transgression, and by no means clearing the guilty, visiting the iniquity of the fathers upon the children unto the third and fourth generation* — Numbers 14:18), and that we need to address real issues and stop dancing and skirting those things that plague our families and us. Women can also discuss the issues facing women. If it is a group that was brought together, say a business person's prayer breakfast, we can really hone in on those areas that can help every one of us individually and collectively address those specific problems.

I believe that it is important that we walk in relationship the way Paul walked in relationship.

First we need to walk in a place of strong covering especially if we are in a place of ministry. Ministerial covering has very little to do in my opinion with administration, rules and regulations and doctrinal affiliations. I believe it has to do with walking in relationship with the person or small group of people whom you share a mutual respect with, a willingness to be open and transparent and it needs to be someone who has every opportunity to speak frankly into areas of our life that may need improvement or correction, as well as encouragement.

Paul had Peter and the council of elders that he willingly submitted himself to. I don't believe we are supposed to force another person to submit to accountability or covering, that must be initiated by the individual himself. Paul, walked in fellowship in three areas, and so should we. First as I mentioned with Peter and the council, second he walked with co-workers or peers into the harvest, as he had Silas and Barnabas. In Luke 10 The Lord sent the seventy out two by two. None of us are designed to be an island. We are to labour together, walk with one another, support one another, and encourage one another.

When I choose to walk with someone I try to make it my business to allow them to speak into my life. I am not looking for their personal critique of my personality or quirks, certainly we all have these. If I choose to walk in unity with another person and they see areas in my life where there is sin, compromise or idolatry, I want them to be able to be open and address those issues. Most of us want to be the best we can be for Christ. Achan's sin affected all of Israel. I want to have a positive affect on those I co-labour with. I would like to have the kind of relationship with my brothers and sisters that if I see something, I could feel free to address it with them. That's what relationship and accountability are about.

This is something that has been sorely missed in the Church. We are even at the point in many situations where we allow people to continue to minister in some leadership capacity, who are walking in open, unrepentant sin, jeopardizing the mission of the whole group. In Proverbs 27:5-6, the Word says, *"open rebuke is better than secret love, and faithful are the wounds of a friend, but the kisses of an enemy are deceitful,"* we need to be open and honest when dealing with one another. In the midst of adversity even at times when our friendship and fellowship are challenged by the truthfulness of our relationship, we can be comforted by Proverbs 17:17, where it says, that *"a friend loveth at all times, and a brother is born for adversity."*

The third area of walking in relationship is in the area of mentorship and discipleship, as Paul walked with Timothy and Titus. An important aspect of the church is that we, who are more mature in faith, begin to take some under our wing. Teaching them the very practical aspect of our walk, sowing into their lives, time, energy and love. We all believe that these are the days of Elijah and he had an Elisha, and even a company of prophets. Malachi 4:5-6, are for now, and the Lord is turning the hearts of the fathers to the children, and the hearts of the children to the fathers.

Let's begin to walk in full relationship, in each of these three areas of our lives. Let's begin to embrace accountability in each of the areas. We all have a blind spot and no matter which way we turn, we can move the blind spot around, but there is always a blind spot that only our brother or sister can see. Whether in a group setting or individual accountability, you may want to ask yourself the following questions on a regular basis. They are written from a male perspective, but come on sisters, put yourselves in the picture. We are all pretty much the same. In God's eyes we are all pretty much the same. I believe He drew the line in Genesis where He made man in His image, both male and female. Then He encouraged us in 1 Corinthians 10:13, that we were all facing very common situations, and he clearly stated, *"There hath no temptation taken you, but such that is common to man, but God is faithful who will not suffer you to be tempted beyond that which you are able, but will with the temptation also make a way to escape, that you may be able to bear it."*

Let us remember that, the victory is ours, the verdict is in and the battle belongs to the Lord!

CHAPTER 3

THE MANDATE OF JESUS AND THE BELIEVER

In this chapter I am going to establish for you the biblical mandate for Jesus and his believers. I am going to take you for a walk in the Word. As many of you know I like to move and live in the glory realm, and in the revelatory realm, and I believe that the further we go in the Spirit, the more solid our biblical foundation needs to be. You can see in almost any stream of ministry today, leaders who were walking in strong truths for many years and moving under the anointing and ministering in the Spirit suddenly drift off into false doctrine, or fall to sin. Many times this comes from beginning to step into revelation or a new realm of ministry without first setting a strong biblical basis and foundation for the revelation and the call that is on your life.

In Isaiah 61:1-4 it clearly gives us the mandate of Messiah.

> *"The Spirit of the Lord GOD is upon Me, Because the LORD has anointed Me to preach good tidings to the poor; He has sent Me to heal the brokenhearted, To proclaim liberty to the captives, And the opening of the prison to those who are bound; ²To proclaim the acceptable year of the LORD, And the day of vengeance of our God; To comfort all who mourn, ³To console those who mourn in Zion, To give them beauty for ashes, The oil of joy for mourning, The garment of praise for the spirit of heaviness; That they may be called trees of righteousness, The planting of the LORD, that He may be glorified." ⁴And they shall rebuild the old ruins, They shall raise up the former*

desolations, And they shall repair the ruined cities, The desolations of many generations."

The Lord said that He was anointed. That God had anointed Him to preach the good news, to bind up the broken hearted, to proclaim liberty to the captive and to release from darkness those that are bound. To proclaim the year of the Lord's favour, to comfort those that mourn. To bring beauty for ashes, to restore the old waste places and former desolations. What a tremendous mandate. That is the prophetic purpose as declared by Isaiah hundreds of years before the birth of Christ. In Luke 4 Jesus was led into the wilderness by the Holy Spirit for His victorious conflict with the evil one. After this victory Luke tells us in 4:16-19,

"[16]So He came to Nazareth, where He had been brought up. And as His custom was, He went into the synagogue on the Sabbath day, and stood up to read. [17]And He was handed the book of the prophet Isaiah. And when He had opened the book, He found the place where it was written: [18]"The Spirit of the LORD is upon Me, Because He has anointed Me To preach the gospel to the poor; He has sent Me to heal the brokenhearted, To proclaim liberty to the captives And recovery of sight to the blind, To set at liberty those who are oppressed; [19]To proclaim the acceptable year of the LORD."

The Word of God tells us that He came to his hometown where He was raised in Nazareth and He went into the synagogue on the Sabbath, which was His custom; and should be ours as well. Let us not forsake the assembly of the brethren and keep the Sabbath holy. He opened the book of Isaiah to the very scripture in Chapter 61:1-4. He read it to them and then He closed the book and said to them in Luke 4:21 *"Today this scripture is fulfilled in your hearing."*

THE MANDATE OF JESUS AND THE BELIEVER

So now, Christ confirms the prophetic mandate given by the prophet Isaiah as His calling. Then we see that He personally walked this out in Matthew 4:23-24 *"²³And Jesus went about all Galilee, teaching in their synagogues, preaching the gospel of the kingdom, and healing all kinds of sickness and all kinds of disease among the people. ²⁴Then His fame went throughout all Syria; and they brought to Him all sick people who were afflicted with various diseases and torments, and those who were demon-possessed, epileptics, and paralytics; and He healed them."*

He preached the gospel of the Kingdom and healed all manner of sickness and disease, cast out demons, set the captive free and healed the broken hearted. Not just there but throughout His whole ministry. You can see that He stayed to his mandate. He answered His call. He preached the Kingdom in Word and demonstrated it in power.

When you look at the very high percentage of ministry encounters, maybe over 30% or so, Jesus ministered deliverance, inner healing and divine physical healing.

He knew that this was not only His mandate, but that He was called to make disciples. To mentor those who followed Him in the same mandate. He said you would know a tree by the fruit it bears, and He bore fruit unto His calling and unto Himself. In Luke Chapter 9:1-2 He called His 12 disciples together and gave them the power and authority to cast out devils and heal diseases and He sent them to preach the kingdom and heal the sick. You may say to me, well Bro. Russ they were the Apostles, and I say to you, they were his disciples.

In Chapter 10, He showed us that it was not just those 12 but He appointed another 70 and sent them out 2 by 2, to do the very same thing. Telling them that the Kingdom of God was near. If that wasn't enough to establish for us that it is the mandate for believers for disciples of Christ, let us go to Mark 16:15-20

> "*[15] And He said to them, "Go into all the world and preach the gospel to every creature. [16] He who believes and is baptized will be saved; but he who does not believe will be condemned. [17] And these signs will follow those who believe: In My name they will cast out demons; they will speak with new tongues; [18] they will take up serpents; and if they drink anything deadly, it will by no means hurt them; they will lay hands on the sick, and they will recover. [19] So then, after the Lord had spoken to them, He was received up into heaven, and sat down at the right hand of God. [20] And they went out and preached everywhere, the Lord working with them and confirming the word through the accompanying signs. Amen."*

This was the mandate that He released to believers on the day of His ascension. He told them to go and do the same thing. You can see He is speaking to them, to believers, not a certain class or title of believers. Are you a believer? I am. So I recognize that He is telling me what I am called to do, which is to emulate the life and the call of Christ. The life and the call of Jesus the Messiah.

In Acts 19 we see in the life of the Apostle Paul who was not one of the original Apostles but by his own confession, one born out of season, like you and I. Born of the Spirit. God did extraordinary miracles through Paul. He even used pieces of his garment in vs. 11 to heal the sick and release them from demonic oppression of evil spirits. He preached the gospel and the bible tells us in Acts 20:19 that the Word of God grew mightily and prevailed.

In Acts 6 the Apostles laid hands on 7 members of their community and named them Deacons, including Stephen who became the first martyr and Philip the Evangelist. They were from among the people. They were just like you and I, pursuing and trying to serve the Lord. Their first call was to serve the Lord and to wait on tables. The bible tells us in Acts 7:8 that Stephen was full of power and did great wonders and miracles among the people. In chapter 8 Philip went to preach the good news in Samaria. In verses 5-8 when God did miracles, unclean spirits cried out in a loud voice and came out of many of them that were possessed. The sick were healed and great joy came to the city. This is our mission; it is our mandate as well as theirs.

Years later in the City of Antioch they began to mock the believers and called them Christians because they were followers of Christ. Christ was not Jesus' last name, but rather meant Jesus, the anointed one. As Christians we are "little Christ's," the anointed ones. We are not only named after him, but are to follow after him, His teachings, His mandate, His call, and His mission.

I wanted to lay this strong foundation so that as you begin to pursue a ministry in warfare in the end time ministry of divine healing and inner healing, you would understand fully and embrace your call. Not wavering to the right or to the left. Not to be influenced by those preaching a happy-go-lucky seeker friendly gospel, but to live as one who understands that the gospel of Christ is preached in Word, demonstrated in power, and is as much a gospel of warfare, confrontation and revolution today, as when He first spoke it and declared it. Sometimes, we all have a tendency to make the life and ministry of Christ into our own likeness according to our own need. Jesus is love; well certainly He is love. He is the God of Love, the essence of love, but He is also the God of righteousness and judgment. Our Jesus opened one of His greatest sermons with "you brood of vipers." He went into the temple observing the moneychangers with a righteous indignation. He went and cut a whip of cords and came back in and turned these tables upside down. He is the same one that knocked Paul off his high horse. The one that you and I are looking for is no longer the babe in the manger. But through a life of conflict and confrontation He defeated the enemies of darkness and He is coming back riding on a white horse with fire in his eyes and a scepter in his hand.

He is the Lord of Hosts, He leads His people in battle. He leads His people to victory.

My prayer for you today is that He would open the eyes of your understanding, that you would know the hope of your calling, that you would embrace the mandate of Christ and the mandate that He gave us. I pray for a fresh anointing and a fresh release of power and authority. Power to heal the sick, to preach the gospel of the Kingdom with great boldness, to cast out demons in His name. To bind up the broken hearted and bring healing and joy to those that mourn.

I ask the Lord to place warrior angels around you and your home, around everything and everyone that is near and dear to you. That the Lord would bless you and empower you and enable you as you pursue your destiny mandate. In Jesus' Name. Amen.

CHAPTER 4

SPIRITUAL WARFARE

The key areas of Christian life and ministry that have to do with spiritual warfare are deliverance, inner healing and intercessory prayer.

I need to understand fully and wholly who I am in Christ and who Christ is in me. One of the most difficult places in my own life and my own call that stood between me and fully answering my call to spiritual warfare was ignorance and wrong teaching.

I know first hand the value of freedom ministry and I know before I can bring liberty and freedom to others, I must have a degree of freedom and victory in my own life. In order for that to happen, I have to begin to answer the question for myself. Do Christians need deliverance? Do I need deliverance? Can a Christian have a demon? Not just from a theological or doctrinal point of view, but from the practical walk and evidence in my life and evidence in others around me.

We as a body do need deliverance, but not just deliverance, we need inner healing as well. We also need to learn to walk together and to walk this liberty out.

DO CHRISTIANS NEED DELIVERANCE?

This is probably one of the most controversial subjects in the Church today. It has been an area of debate and disagreement for many years. I am going to attempt, in this chapter to clearly cover this subject from a biblical standpoint and from a point of personal experience and practical observation. In the end, each one of us will have to come to our own conclusion on the entirety of the subject. All I ask of you as we examine this subject together, is that you keep an open mind and lay aside all pre-conceived notions, traditions and doctrines that have been passed down to you, so that we can take an unbiased look at probably one of the most serious subjects facing the end time Church.

Let me begin by saying to you that I don't believe that any born again believer, can be demon-possessed. I believe that man is a triune being — spirit, soul and body. At the time that we accept Jesus Christ as our Lord and Saviour and believe in our heart that God raised Jesus from the dead according to Romans 10:9-10, we are saved. I believe that our spirits are born again from a place of carnality, and possessed by the Lord Jesus Christ fully and completely. No ifs, ands, no buts. When the Son of God possesses our spirits, Satan can't possess them as well!

Our soul on the other hand, is renewed or sanctified by the washing of the water of the Word. In my opinion, this is not an instantaneous action, but the process of sanctification is a life-long pursuit. Our soul is made up of mind, will and emotions and I believe it comes into conformity on each of those levels by a daily process of crucifying the flesh and submission of our will to the Will of God.

If the Lord waited for every evil spirit to leave our minds before we got saved, it would seem to me, we would have to be saved moments before He took us to be with Him. Think about that. Think about your own situation, perhaps you were like me.

I was in the world. I was living a life full of sin and self. At the time that I got saved in 1976, I had problems with alcohol, drugs, elicit sex, gambling, cursing, etc., etc., etc. Maybe you were morally sound, but me, my life was a mess when Jesus Christ in all His mercy and all His grace decided to reveal His plan of salvation to me. Maybe, like me, you had a lot of problems, but the next day you were instantly made holy in thought, word and deed. In my case, I became aware of my sin and He began a process of sanctification that included personal deliverance.

It was a day-by-day, sometimes even hour-by-hour, even moment-by-moment battle. The enemy did not want to give up the ground that he'd taken in my life, and my physical body went through a form of withdrawal and didn't want to give up easy. I don't know about you, this is thirty-five years later and he's still trying to do battle with me. I'm happy to tell you, that due to the power and the guidance of the Holy Spirit and the ministry of deliverance, I am walking in victory, living a victorious life!

According to the Word, we'll have these same bodies until we're glorified. My body still fights, so does my soul, but at the beginning the battle was more intense and difficult because in addition to the desires of the flesh and due to sins and generational curses, I had opened myself up to evil spirits. The personal deliverance that the Lord took me through occurred on a number of occasions during the first sixty days I was saved. It was like peeling an onion. He took off layer after layer of these hindering spirits that were harassing and tormenting me.

Let me share with you my experience, and I know, with every individual it's different. I was unchurched and got saved reading the Bible in my home. My deliverance occurred in two ways. First, at times I was praying I would see vividly in a vision in my mind's eye a particular behaviour pattern. While I repented, a spirit of weeping and travail would come over me for a period and then a release of pressure. As the spirit left, I felt a change of emotion and countenance, and then a relief.

Other times, I'd get a lump that felt like the size of a grapefruit, tighten up in my stomach and it would bring me such pain. Again this occurred in the privacy of my room during times of prayer and fellowship with the Lord. The pain would get so excruciating that all I could do was lie on the floor on my stomach and roll back and forth until I felt relief. Sometimes, I'd burp or sneeze as I was rolling and there would be a release, I'd feel relief and my stomach would be soft again.

Most of the time in my spirit, while the pain was coming on me, that small still voice that first brought me to salvation told me exactly what spirit was causing this pain; anger, jealousy, addiction, etc. It took a little while, but He cleaned me up. During these past 35 years, I have had occasions in my life for spirits to come back in, and on many of those occasions, similar to the first time, the Lord would take me through a form of self-deliverance.

At other times I've had other ministers pray for me until healing and deliverance came. Now, you've heard my personal experience of how I was already saved yet still needed deliverance. Let's look at a couple of biblical examples.

Let's look at Acts 8, where Phillip went to the City of Samaria and people with unclean spirits cried out in a loud voice and the spirits came out of many of them. In verse 9-13 a man named Simon, a sorcerer, was converted, for it says he believed in verse 13 and in that same verse the Bible tells us he was baptized and began to walk with Philip. After some time had passed, Peter and John, when they had heard the news, came to the city and began laying hands on the new believers and they received the Holy Ghost. In verses 18-19 Simon, when he saw this power, wanted it and offered money and was rebuked by Peter. In verse 22, he was told to repent and pray that God would forgive him, and in verse 23, Peter perceived in the Spirit that, he (Simon) had the spirit of a gall of bitterness in him and was in the bond of iniquity. This was after he was saved and baptized.

Let's look to Acts 5:3, Ananias who was a born again follower and most of you know he even sold his property and gave a portion of the proceeds to the church, but lied to the Holy Spirit by saying he was giving it all. Peter again through revelation of the Holy Spirit stated that Satan filled his heart with lies and deceit. Ananias paid along with his wife Sapphira with their lives for this breach.

I could go on and on citing biblical examples, but just one more; Peter in his first epistle which was written for

God's elect and deals almost throughout with a message to Christians dealing with godly living, in Chapter 5:8-9 tells us we must be vigilant and not open up the door to the enemy, the devil, because the same afflictions that are to the world are to the brothers.

When we look at the ministry of deliverance we need only look to the life of Christ — our example — the author and the finisher of our faith. His ministry, according to biblical accounts, had a high percentage (maybe one quarter of His ministry) of activity spent in deliverance. In Mark chapter 16, on the day of His ascension, He spoke in verse 15-20 directly to His disciples the Great Commission and in verse 17 He said, *"and these signs shall follow them that believe, in my name, shall they cast out devils."* Hallelujah!

DO I NEED DELIVERANCE?

As I told you in one of the previous chapters, most of the people for whom I provide personal ministry and deliverance are Christian leaders, pastors, Christian workers and their families, people on the move trying to do something for God. Any of us, and I would venture to say most of us need deliverance and personal ministry. We need to rid ourselves of related demonic spirits.

Do we really need deliverance? Maybe not, if you've lived a life of purity and holiness, if you've never had any addictive behaviour, illicit sexual activity, no relationship problems with family, friends and leaders and if your family tree stands blameless and holy as you do. And of course, everyone in your family line was a tither, so you haven't fallen under the curse of poverty. Now, if that is really you, then you are just fine. If you are living that victorious Christian life right now, living in that place and walking in the Glory, under proper spiritual authority and in the proper alignment with nothing hindering your prayer life . . . say Hallelujah!

Let's look realistically and seriously at this question. "Do I need deliverance?" I feel the following are some signs that may tell you if the deliverance ministry could help you. Deliverance is not a substitute for a dedicated and consecrated Christian walk. If your prayer life is in order, you're in the Word every day and you're trying to live a life that expresses good Christian and biblical morals and values, but there are things in this following list that are in some way affecting your life, then I feel you should consider personal deliverance ministry.

1. Are you struggling with any addictive behaviour patterns; smoking, drinking, sexual behaviour or eating disorders?

2. Are you being plagued by depression and oppression repetitively and do these bouts seem to drain you of all your energy, or cause you to be incapable of handling your normal routine?

3. Do you find yourself apologizing often or experiencing emotional outbursts that seem to be uncontrollable, such as anger, crying etc.?

4. When you lose a loved one or terminate a primary relationship in your life, there is a normal season of grieving that is necessary and healthy. However, if you find that you are grieving months, even years later, this traumatic experience in your life may have opened you up to a spirit of grief, mourning and depression and deliverance ministry may be of great help.

5. Were you, or your parents, or your grandparents ever involved with witchcraft, the occult, ESP or fraternal organizations that participated in secret oath taking, experiences such as the Masonic lodge, Eastern Star, Job's daughters, or were you ever involved in a cult or some Eastern religion, yoga or meditation?

6. If during the night you are tormented by bad dreams or nightmares, involving violence, bloodshed, murder, perversion or sexual impurity, that's a sign that something that is not good or not of God is going on in the realm of your subconscious. I'm not talking about just one bad dream but rather a pattern of them. That's also not saying that God doesn't occasionally use negative dreams to communicate with us especially for intercession.

7. Do you suffer from sicknesses that also plagued your parents or grandparents?

This gives you a good idea and certainly this is not a complete list. Personal ministry or deliverance and inner healing would be beneficial for you if you related to any of these questions. I know it has been a life changing experience for me and many of the people I've been associated with over the years. Sometimes, due to past abuse in the deliverance ministry or through wrong teaching or through denial on our part, we shy away from the very thing that can help us the most. If you feel you need deliverance, please feel free to contact our office or someone in your area who operates in the deliverance ministry.

After I receive my freedom and liberty or at least a degree thereof (and remember, I believe it is an ongoing quest and not just to be free but also to stay free and live free), then I can begin to bring freedom to others.

The Lord wants us to embark on this ministry and life. If you look at Mark 9:38-40, *"[38] John said to Him, Teacher, we saw someone casting out demons in Your name, and we tried to prevent him because he was not following us.' [39] But Jesus said, "Do not hinder him, for there is no one who will perform a miracle in My name, and be able soon afterward to speak evil of Me. [40] For he who is not against us is or us.'"* John the revelator was talking about those other ministries who were not part of their particular company. In other words they were with other denominations or fellowships down the street and they were casting out demons.

John said that the disciples forbade them to do so, but in vs. 39 Jesus tells him not to forbid them to do that. He also called it a miracle and said people who performed a miracle in His name would find it difficult to speak against Him. Not only are we called to live free, but the call that was on the life of Christ in Isaiah 60:1 is the call and mandate that is on our life in Mark 16. It is a sign and a wonder and a miracle.

Let's just take one more perspective, and observe the Church of Jesus Christ. I travel and get an opportunity to speak in many churches and I see people who are saved, born again believers, many baptized in water and the Holy Spirit, who some 10, 15, 20 years later are still tormented and harassed in their minds both in the day and in the night by demonic activity; some still carrying baggage such as lust, rejection, fear, phobias, uncontrolled anger and infirmities. I'm not saying all, but many of these probably stem from demonic activity operating within their bodies and souls tormenting and harassing them and keeping them from enjoying the victorious life of their Christianity.

In the last 15 years, I have personally been involved in over 400 individual deliverance sessions and countless numbers in group settings and corporate meetings. Most of the people who received personal ministry were church leaders, Pastors, Christian workers and their families. In upwards of 95% of these deliverance sessions many demonic spirits manifested in numerous ways and expelled or left the individual with obvious evidence, such as sneezing, burping, yawning, etc.

The testimonies of changed lives, and new victorious walks after receiving deliverance and inner healing were phenomenal. It is a wonderful ministry and it is truly miraculous to see a person walk in oppressed and heavily tormented and leave in joy and freedom and liberty. Their new countenance makes it very rewarding. It may be a bit messy, a bit controversial and certainly with some persecution, but very rewarding. *It's not by power, nor by might, but by my Spirit saith the Lord* (Zech. 4:6). You make up your mind, but I can tell you this, a man with a personal experience is never at the mercy of the man with a good argument. Hallelujah!

Father, I pray right now that the anointing and impartation for freedom ministry and deliverance would be released upon the life of these readers, that they would have a strong desire to see people walking in freedom and maintaining their freedom and stepping out to see the captive set free! In Jesus' Name. Amen!

CHAPTER 5

INNER HEALING

Part of the journey to freedom that is available to every Christian according to the purposes and mandates of Christ is inner healing. He came to bind up the broken hearted as well as to set the captive free. I believe that this journey begins first and foremost with recognizing my present condition of bondage or need; recognizing that I am being wrongly influenced by demonic spirits, as well as past negative experiences in my life. Then I need the ministry of deliverance to rid myself of this demonic oppression.

For a long time, that was as far as I was able to go in my own understanding. Once myself or another individual had been set free I thought that was the end of the experience. But I realized that many people who had been set free were not able to stay free. That for a variety of reasons or circumstances they would fall back into wrong thought or behaviour patterns that reopened the door and again allowed demonic activity to operate and negatively influence their lives.

I had a negative outlook on counseling in the Christian community based on seeing individuals who were not properly trained or equipped and credentialed, who were counseling individuals in what certainly appeared to be a less than professional manner. I have gone through some major personal negative experiences and I have benefited from professional counseling. I also personally benefited from wonderful pastoral care given me by my Pastor, Paul Wetzel, and others in the Christian community.

It was actually the mixture of both that troubled me. I have come to believe now that many people do need professional counseling. Sometimes concerning their marriage or finances, relationships or addiction. Many times, that counseling needs to be done by a professional who is trained and accredited to do that. But at times we also need spiritual care and ministry from a pastor or mentor in our life to deal with spiritual issues. They can, during deliverance or prayer for inner healing, give us spiritual understanding concerning the root causes of our problems so that we will know how to walk out our freedom. We need to close the door to sin and iniquity in our life.

As I mentioned I was not really a big believer in inner healing, but the Lord sent a wonderful young lady into my life who had a great anointing for inner healing. Her name is Patricia Thorpe Wallace. She also became my assistant and administrator for Eagle Worldwide Ministries. Because of our close professional relationship and her sensitive nature, I knew she was anointed and I allowed her to pray for some people who were experiencing ongoing problems. She would pray and identify the root causes of these behaviours and influences and sometimes explain to them how to avoid the pitfalls of reoccurring issues, and the results made me a believer.

People were able to not only break the cycle and chains and bondages but now I saw them become stronger and able to maintain and walk out their freedom. I realized that this is part of the process and journey of freedom. I began to allow her to do training courses comprised of six to eight sessions, teaching, prayer ministry and practical application of the gospel of Jesus Christ into the broken areas of their lives.

These seminars and prayer times dealt with subjects such as how our families, our mothers, our fathers, and/or authority figures in our lives caused wounding in our life. She taught on judgments and dishonor, vows, and bitter-root expectancy and brought healing to areas like shame, lies, hurt and pain. The entire process brought us a great deal of lasting fruit.

The Word of God tells us to take an axe to the root. By learning to deal with these root causes, people were better able to deal with the real life issues that they were being confronted with, consequently maintaining their liberty and freedom.

Again, I am very comfortable with the style of pastoral care and ministry, which includes training and prayer, but there are also areas of inner healing that I would not necessarily recommend that I have experienced and have seen some problems reoccurring. Some of them concern ongoing counseling that in many cases leads to just another form of co-dependency between the individual and the counselor. This is just another kind of bondage. I don't necessarily agree with some of the areas or types of inner healing that include spirit guides and theophostic ministry. I have seen some good and poor results from that style of ministry and I would be very cautious to recommend it because the positive or negative results are based highly on the ministerial ability of the facilitator.

One area where I have seen people work with positive results in these styles of inner healing is when you are dealing with some of the more difficult cases such as disassociated identity disorder and satanic ritual abuse. I believe as we get deeper into the harvest, we are going to have to learn to deal increasingly with these difficult specialty situations because many of them are birthed through problems and circumstances, such as rape and molestation, prostitution, serious prolonged and profound drug addiction, satanic and ritualistic religions and cults.

If you happen to be dealing or ever need training and knowledge or information concerning individuals troubled in the ways that I have mentioned, the person that I actually consider a true authority in these areas is Bill Sudduth. He is the President of the International Society of Deliverance Ministers and is under the spiritual covering of C. Peter Wagner and Doris Wagner. He graduated from the Brownsville School of Ministry and in my opinion, is one of the leading authorities on deliverance and inner healing. His offices are located in Colorado Springs, Colorado. The organization that he heads up is the largest group of recognized deliverance ministers in the world.

Let me close this chapter by saying I sincerely recommend that you do not begin to do deliverance or inner healing ministry without having the proper spiritual covering, training and guidance necessary and when you do, be sure to stay in the area of expertise that you are qualified for.

Be sure you have the proper prayer covering, that you don't work alone but have a helper and facilitator with you as well as an intercessor and that any individuals that are receiving this ministry from you realize the extent of your training and ministry. Counseling should be done by qualified and accredited counselors. Pastoral care should be done by ministers. Health care, physical and mental problems should be attended to by physicians, psychologists and psychiatrists.

God uses many different means and individuals to achieve His purpose of healing and freedom in our lives. My prayer for you is that the Lord would anoint you to heal the broken hearted, to bring liberty to the captive that He would release to you a Spirit of wisdom and counsel that you may use to bless many of His sons and daughters as we stand and advance His Kingdom. In Jesus Name. Amen.

CHAPTER 6

SIN, CURSES AND UNFORGIVENESS

Here are some other hindrances in my quest for freedom dealing with the power of words.

Sins, curses and unforgiveness are three of the most prominent areas of our lives that open doors in our life to demonic attack and activity.

In this chapter, I want to take these areas and talk about each one of them. I hope that the awareness of each area will give us the opportunity to go back and close doors that we may become overcomers!

SIN

Let's start with SIN. For all too long the word holiness has been a dirty word in the Church, and brought to our minds thoughts of legalism. Holiness has almost nothing to do with how we dress or the way we look. Holiness is a posture of our hearts and the Lord looks upon the condition of our hearts. Just as there were Pharisees of old there are Pharisees today. They know just how to dress, how to act, they have all the right amens and hallelujahs. They sit in the right seat in the Church and they know how to say all the long prayers in public. They know how to make everyone think they are holy. The thing that made them so angry with Jesus back then, still does now. He saw right through them and He told them that they were hypocrites. He was not afraid to reveal the condition of their hearts. The Lord called sin, sin and so must we, if we call ourselves followers of Christ.

If we're doing spiritual warfare and we are, whether we like it or not and whether we recognize it or not, we must know the enemy, and the enemy of God is SIN! If it is God's enemy than it must also be our enemy. The sin of the world is my enemy and I hate it, but more than that I must have a holy hatred for my own sin. Repetitive and unrepentant sins are open doors, invitations for the enemy to attack my mind and body. I must put it all under the blood. I must repent. Repentance is the great gift of God. We are all sinners, every one of us fall short of the Glory of God. The psalmist said in Psalm 24, that he who ascends the hill of God, MUST have clean hands and a pure heart.

There is no way for us to be holy except through the guidance of the Holy Spirit, a humble heart and contrite spirit and God's gift to me, the gift of repentance. The Word says in 1 John 1:9, that if I am faithful to confess my sin then He is faithful to forgive me of my sins and cleanse me from all unrighteousness.

It seems like we complicate everything when the Christian walk is ever so simple. I didn't say easy, I said simple. Like identifying sin, SIN is anything that Jesus wouldn't do! Sin is watching something on TV that you couldn't watch in church on Sunday morning. Sin is as much on the inside as it is on the outside. It seems like we are quick, just like the Pharisees, to point the finger at the adulteress, drug addict, alcoholic or prostitute but there is no big or little sin. Sin is Sin, and sin separates us from God! It was murmuring and complaining that kept the Israelites from the peace and prosperity of the Promised Land and it's sin that will keep us from the promise of God on our life. It is the gossip, judging, backbiting, mocking and criticisms. It's ALL sin.

Let's take a moment now and allow the Holy Spirit to search our hearts.

Holy Spirit, search me in your mercy, reveal my sin, my shortcomings and the iniquities of my heart. I repent for every time I hurt others, for the times I hurt you, the times I hurt those I love and for the times I hurt myself. I ask you now, to wash away my sin, my pain and my shame with the blood that Jesus shed for the forgiveness of my sin.

UNFORGIVENESS

Unforgiveness is sin. It opens the door for the enemy to attack us. Unforgiveness almost always results in resentment and bitterness and allows demonic spirits to operate against us. When we fail to give forgiveness it may also bring a curse against us. In Mark 11:25, the Word tells us that if we have anything against anyone, to forgive and that our Father in heaven will forgive us.

In my experience with personal deliverance, I have found unforgiveness to be the number one spirit that blocks deliverance. I've found that almost every one of us have had some very difficult and painful experiences in the area of relationship. Some in our childhood, some in our marriages, some in the Church. More often than not this pain was inflicted upon us by those we loved and cared about the most. Those that we gave access to our heart, and I've found in most cases, that they are the most difficult to forgive. Forgiveness is a choice we make, an act of our will, an act of love. The person who we feel is at fault can't earn our forgiveness. We must freely give it. They can't earn it any more than we can earn it from God. He forgives from a heart of love, so must we.

Unforgiveness chokes the blessings of God. It chokes our faith. In Mark 11:23-25, it is no accident that the forgiveness verse follows the verse on application of faith. There are no accidents in the Word of God, it's by design. Unforgiveness opens the door to unbelief and chokes our faith.

Without faith it is impossible to please God and makes us unable to receive from Him. Think about it, everything we receive from God, we receive by faith. Salvation, healing, the baptism in the Holy Spirit etc. If unforgiveness breeds unbelief and unbelief is the opposite of faith, then unforgiveness chokes off all the blessings of God in our life. We must forgive those who offend us more for ourselves, than we do for them. It hurts them, but look at all the ways unforgiveness works against us.

If there are some people that you find difficult to forgive in certain circumstances or situations and it still brings you pain when you think about them, then you need to pray this prayer with me and make the conscious decision now to forgive, not just for their sake but for Christ's sake and not just for His sake but for your sake.

Lord, I have a confession to make: I have not always loved, but have resented certain people and have unforgiveness in my heart, and I call upon you, Lord, to help me forgive them. It is my will and desire to forgive them from my heart. I don't know if I can, but I want to. I ask you to help me forgive them and take all of the hurt and pain away. I do now forgive (name them, both living and dead) and ask you to forgive them also, Lord. I do now forgive and accept myself, in the name of Jesus Christ.

CURSES

We could write a whole book on curses but for the sake of time I'm going to cover what I feel are three of the most predominant types.

The world book dictionary defines curse — as to ask God to bring evil or harm on, as in Exodus 22:28 or to bring evil or harm such as torment. World's Bible Dictionary by Don Hemming states that cursing in the Hebrew word was not a burst of bad language as it usually is in the world today. From a biblical perspective it is a pronouncement of judgment, believed to bring the release of powerful forces against the person or persons cursed (Num 22:6, Judges 5:23, Job 31:30, Prov 30:10).

SIN, CURSES AND UNFORGIVENESS

Let's talk first about generational curses found in Exodus 34:6-7, as the Lord clearly proclaimed His name and His ways to Moses on Mt. Sinai *"And the Lord passed by before him, and proclaimed, The Lord, the Lord God, merciful and gracious, longsuffering, and abundant in goodness and truth. Keeping mercy for thousands, forgiving iniquity and transgression and sin, and that will by no means clear the guilty; visiting the iniquity of the fathers upon the children, and upon the children's children, unto the third and to the fourth generation."*

A perfect example of this is King David. In his sin of adultery, sexual impurity with Bathsheba, God forgave him, clearly God forgave him but the child died. You can look down through the generations at the children of David and see the far-reaching consequences of David's sin. David was a man after God's own heart. God loved David, but God is not a respecter of persons.

His law is **THE** Law. We can see this same scenario in most contemporary families. I see it all the time. It shows up in the area of sin going from generation to generation, such as alcoholism, drug use, physical abuse, divorce and poverty. When we defy the law of God we pass the consequences down upon our children and our children's children. Is there no way out? Didn't Christ take the curse of the law on Himself on the cross? Certainly He did, He is the way out. Like everything He won for us at the cross, He did not make it so everyone in the world would be saved, but only by those appropriating that blessing and taking the prescribed action of receiving by faith and proclaiming it, are they saved (Romans 10:9, 10).

The law also won for us our healing. *"By His stripes we are healed,"* yet we need to receive it by faith and take the appropriate action described in James 5:14-15. It's the same in the area of deliverance. All three of these were accomplished at the cross. The Greek word Sozo means healed, saved and delivered. So it is with deliverance from curses and evil spirits. We must repent of the sin, our own and those of our fore fathers, breaking the curses and sending them back. According to Mark 16:15-20 cast out the evil spirits and related spirits.

If you know that there was sin and iniquity in your family line or in your own life, then I would like you to pray this prayer with me.

In the name of Jesus Christ, I repent of all of the sins and iniquities of my mother and father and their mothers and fathers back 15 generations that allowed demon spirits and curses to pass into me. I specifically repent of the sins and iniquities that allowed the demon spirits of rejection, bitterness, depression, fear, guilt, grief, infirmities, and lust and their nests or families to pass into me when I was conceived. I renounce all of those demons and I break every curse that allows those spirits to remain within me and I put them under the blood of Jesus Christ who took upon himself according to Galatians 3:13 and became a curse of the law for me. I renounce and loose from myself all of the resulting curses and connected spirits and cancel them in the Name of Jesus. I ask you God to bless all of my remaining family line.

O God, I confess to you the iniquities of my father, and I ask You to forgive him. I confess that my grandfather and my great grandfather were workers of iniquity and held it in their hearts, and I ask You to forgive them. And I forgive them. Lord I confess to You that I have iniquity in my heart. I ask You to forgive my iniquity [name them] *and remove them from me.*

O God, I confess to the Financial Iniquity of my father, and I ask you to forgive him. I confess that my grandfather and great grandfather were workers of Financial Iniquity, and I ask You to forgive them. Lord, I confess to you that I have Financial Iniquity in my heart. I renounce it and ask you to forgive my iniquity and remove it from me. Thank you, Lord Jesus.

Well, well, well. You know as soon as we start talking about curses, demons, and evil spirits all of a sudden we're a ghost buster. We need to do spiritual warfare, we need to recognize the enemy, and we need to do battle. The Lord says in Matthew 11:12 *"And from the days of John the Baptist until now the kingdom of heaven has suffered violence, and the violent take it by force."* It's time to take off the gloves, time to get down to business.

We have inside of us, all the power we need. We have inside of us the Holy Ghost. Most of the time we walk around rubbing shoulders with the enemy, all lovey dovey. You would think the Holy Ghost in us is Casper the friendly ghost. **Come on Church**, time to get real, time to do battle, time to do war! There's a sound going out in all the earth, the trumpet sounding. Listen, listen close, it's the battle cry of the Lord. He's calling forth the warriors from the North, South, East and West. This is the time that all the prophets prophesied about, the time of the great battle, the day and the hour of the great victory. Arise Church this is your day and this is the hour!

JUDGEMENTS

From my own experience and observations I've made as I visit other churches, one of the areas where we as Christians cause ourselves damage, is in the area of criticism and judgment. In the fall of 1999 while working at a Carlos Annocondia Crusade with Joan Gieson in Orlando, Florida, the Lord ministered to me in a vision, concerning this area of judgment.

In the vision I saw a long judges bench and walking out from behind the bench I saw the Supreme Court Justices of the United States, but they were all midgets. You couldn't really see them till they came out the end. They came out the right side of the bench. They had large heads and the body of a midget and were hand cuffed together. When I ask the

Lord for the interpretation, this is what I received. They were coming out on the right of the bench, which is moving in the flesh. Because they were judges it meant they were making judgment in the flesh. Their heads were big which told me many of the judgments we make are caused by a spirit of pride (big headed). The justices, as a whole, represent the Church. They were hand cuffed together because, when we judge one another it causes both of us to be bound, the person judged and the one pronouncing the judgment. He showed me that they were midgets because when we judge, we stunt our own growth.

Many times we make these judgments, criticize, accuse or mock from a place of ignorance and pride. For whatever reason, if this is an area of your life that needs attention, now is the time, not just to stop it but to get a handle on it every day. Let's pray!

Heavenly Father, I repent of all the judgments I have made against other people including my mother, father, spouse, children, friends, pastors and political leaders. I realize they are sin and can result in curses against me. I ask you to forgive me and I ask you to bless all of the people I have ever judged. I break all of the curses involved and I put them under the blood of Jesus and cancel all related and connected spirits.

WORD CURSES

Ouch, did you say word curses? YES! In James 3:8, we are told about taming our tongue. It says that the tongue is unruly and evil, full of deadly poison. We know that the tongue can bring both blessing and cursing. With the tongue we praise our Lord and Father, and with it we curse men who have been made in God's likeness. Out of the same mouth come praise (blessings) and curses. My brothers, this should not be. Can both fresh water and salt water flow from the same spring? My brothers, can a fig tree bear olives or a grapevine bear figs? Neither can a salt spring produce fresh water.

Oh, the tongue. We use it on others, we use it on ourselves and others use theirs on us. For some of us, the problems we are experiencing right now are the results of word curses spoken over us by parents or other loved ones, even in our childhood. There is power both positive and negative in the words we speak. They bring both pain and gain. Some of these things were spoken in anger, haste or ignorance.

Some things spoken in our childhood cause negative thoughts to bounce around in our minds, causing us great pain, robbing us of energy, causing depression, low self esteem, lack of initiative and hopelessness, along with a host of other negative thoughts and behavior patterns. Maybe someone you loved or respected did this to you. Maybe you did this to one of your children, or someone you cared about. Those idle words we say without thinking, "You'll never learn, you're stupid, you'll never amount to much" etc. Oh, the words we say!

What we need to do is take the steps to correct the damage already done and take the fresh revelation we've received on the blessings and the cursing of our words to correct the negative behaviour patterns in the future. First things first, let's plead the blood over ourselves and our loved ones and break these curses off along with all related spirits. Pray blessings over ourselves and our families and do not delay, DO IT now!

Heavenly Father, I plead the precious blood of Jesus over the hearts and minds of myself, family, children and loved ones and I repent for every negative word I have spoken over anyone. I ask you Father to forgive anyone who has spoken word curses over me. I ask you to forgive them. In the name of Jesus, I now rebuke, break and loose myself and my children from any and all evil curses, and I cancel all connected and related spirits and command them to leave me and my family now. I thank you Lord for setting me free.

OUR WORDS

The Power of life and death,
Lies in the words we choose to say
We can darken the situation,
Or, brighten the worst of days.

Our words bring grace and healing
Or, trouble and despair,
We can speak the truth in love,
Or, in anger be unfair.

We can choose to build up and edify
Or, tear down and abuse,
Disrespect and disregard,
Or, walk a mile in their shoes.

Do we speak to bring encouragement?
Or, do our words make us the judge?
Are we humble and admit it
Or, does pride not let us budge?

Does the past dictate the present?
Do we repeat the same old views?
Do we speak to things a new way?
Or, do we belittle and accuse?

Do we manipulate in silence,
Refusing now to speak?
Demanding things go our way
Or, is it His will that we seek.

Do we speak words of peace?
Or add fuel to the fire of strife?
In the words we speak to others
Do we bring death or life?

CHAPTER 7

PRAYER AND INTERCESSION

As I have mentioned before, intercession and prayer are two of the primary ministry calls and purposes having to do with spiritual warfare, and prophetic intercession is one of the 12 realms of prophecy.

As described in Jeremiah 27:18-22

"[18]But if they are prophets, and if the word of the LORD is with them, let them now entreat the LORD of hosts that the vessels which are left in the house of the LORD, in the house of the king of Judah and in Jerusalem may not go to Babylon. [19]For thus says the LORD of hosts concerning the pillars, concerning the sea, concerning the stands and concerning the rest of the vessels that are left in this city, [20]which Nebuchadnezzar king of Babylon did not take when he carried into exile Jeconiah the son of Jehoiakim, king of Judah, from Jerusalem to Babylon, and all the nobles of Judah and Jerusalem. [21]Yes, thus says the LORD of hosts, the God of Israel, concerning the vessels that are left in the house of the LORD and in the house of the king of Judah and in Jerusalem, [22]'They will be carried to Babylon and they will be there until the day I visit them,' declares the LORD. 'Then I will bring them back and restore them to this place.'"

Here He said, if I am a prophet and the Word of the Lord is with me, then I am called to make intercession and He says in verse 18, to make intercession now. He tells me who to make intercession to: the Lord of Hosts. He didn't say to pray and intercede to the babe in the manger, but actually to the one who is the Lord of Hosts — our leader in battle, the triumphant and victorious one.

He tells me what to intercede for. First, the Word says to intercede for those that remain in the house of the Lord so they will not go back to Babylon, which is a place of captivity and confusion. Then intercede for the leaders, the pillars, the king and the worshippers, the house of Judah. Intercede for the multitude of people, for the unsaved and also for the outreach centers and para-church organizations and also to pray for those that are in my city with the heart of my prayer as in vs. 22; that the Lord would bring restoration in all things.

TYPES OF PRAYER

There are many different types and styles of prayer. This chapter focuses on intercession, particularly prophetic intercession. I would like to describe and give some scripture references regarding different types and styles of prayer.

REPETITIVE PRAYER

Some individuals hold to the principle that any prayer that is recited or repeated regularly is not good. They believe only free style, free flowing prayer is acceptable. Personally, there are a number of prayers that I pray regularly, one being a daily prayer covering. There are many Christians, sincere Christians, that pray the "Our Father," and I do not feel there is anything wrong with that. However, I do not offer that up in my own personal prayer life, for I feel that the Lord was teaching his disciples a formula and a foundation for prayer, a "how-to" if you will.

I believe Jesus spoke the "Lord's prayer" in John 17:20-21, when He said, *"Neither pray I for these alone, but for them also which shall believe on Me through their word; That they all may be one; as Thou, Father, art in Me, and I in Thee, that they also may be one in Us: that the world may believe that Thou has sent Me."*

PRAYER OF PETITION

Certainly we can go overboard here, but we all have our prayer requests and petitions. We all have our little shopping lists. A few of the most important factors for me as I'm petitioning the Father are:

1. That I don't focus these prayers on just me and mine, you know, my brother, my sister-in-law, my nephew and their little doggie "Spot."

2. The Word tells us to pray "as though it were" (Romans 4:17), making positive proclamations and thanking Him for the answer before we see it. We believe we receive, WHEN we pray.

3. It is important we pray the prayers of petition with persistence, determination, and diligence and most importantly with faith, according to the instructions in the Word of God. When we do we can be confident that what we pray according to His will shall be done.

PROPHETIC INTERCESSION

In prophetic intercession, the object is to pray the heart and desires of God. This is praying by the Spirit, in the Spirit as outlined in Romans 8:26-27 *"Likewise the Spirit also helpeth our infirmities for we know not what we should pray for as we ought; but the Spirit itself maketh intercession for us with groanings which cannot be uttered. Also He that searcheth the hearts knoweth which is the mind of the Spirit, because He maketh intercession for the saints according to the will of God."*

PRAISE

We do warfare through worship. This is how we overcome, as outlined in Psalm 8:1-2, *"O Lord, our Lord, how majestic is your name in all the earth! You have set your glory above the heavens, from the lips of children and infants; you have ordained praise because of your enemies to silence the foe and the avenger."* In this way, we silence the voice of the enemy. Ruth Heflin in her best selling book, Glory, describes praise and worship ever so well. She states that we praise until the spirit of worship comes, then we are to worship until the glory comes and then stand in the glory. It is in the glory realm, that wonderful manifest presence of God, that all things are possible. It is in the glory where miracles occur, provision is made for us and that revelation is received, and we may truly soar to spiritual heights in prayer.

PRAYER OF AGREEMENT

The Word tells us that one can put a thousand to flight and two can put ten thousand to flight (Deuteronomy 32:30). Jesus also promises in Matthew 18:19, *"That if two of you shall agree on earth as touching anything, that they shall ask and it shall be done for them of My Father which is in heaven."*

PRAYER FOR THE SICK

Certainly this is a prayer of intercession and a prayer of faith and praise as described in James 5:13-16 *"Is any among you afflicted? Let him pray. Is there any merry? Let him sing psalms. Is there any sick among you? Let him call for the elders of the church; and let them pray over him, anointing him with oil in the name of the Lord. And the prayer of faith shall save the sick, and the Lord shall raise him up; and if he hath committed sins, they shall be forgiven him. Confess your faults one to another, and pray for one another that ye may be healed. The effectual fervent prayer of a righteous man availeth much."*

PRAYER FOR YOUR ENEMIES

The Lord made it very clear for us that He wants us to pray not only for our friends but also for our enemies. In Matthew 5:43 Jesus says, *"You have heard that it was said, love your neighbour and hate your enemy, but I tell you love your enemies and pray for those who persecute you, that you may be sons of your Father in heaven. He causes His sun to rise on the evil and the good, and sends rain on the righteous and the unrighteous. If you love those who love you, what reward will you get? Are not even the tax collectors doing that? And if you greet only your brothers, what are you doing more than others? Do not even the pagans do that? Be perfect, therefore as your heavenly Father is perfect."*

PRAYING IN THE SPIRIT (PRAYING IN TONGUES)

1 Corinthians 14:14 says, *"For if I pray in a tongue my spirit prays, but my mind is unfruitful, so what shall I do? I will pray with my spirit but I will also pray with my mind; I will sing with my spirit but I will also sing with my mind."* Acts 2:4 says, *"And they were all filled with the Holy Spirit and began to speak in other tongues as the Spirit gave them utterance.* Paul tells us in 1 Corinthians 14:4, that he who *"speaks in a tongue edifies himself."* In verse 18 he said, *"I thank God that I speak in tongues more than all of you."*

PRAYER FOR THE NATIONS

Psalm 2:8 says, *"Ask of Me and I will make the nations your inheritance, the ends of the earth your possession. You will rule them with an iron scepter; you will dash them to pieces like pottery."* In the Great Commission, Matthew 28:18, the Lord shows us His heart for lost souls and the harvest. We need to allow that vision and commandment to be fulfilled through us in our prayer life, and pray diligently for the nations.

The Word of God tells us that our churches are to be houses of prayer. Jesus said in Matthew 21:13 *"It is written, my house shall be called a house of prayer."* No matter what type or style of prayer, the object is to make ourselves a house of prayer and to pray without ceasing, that we would be men and women of prayer. So often we've fought for prayer in our schools, government buildings and meetings. We need to begin to stand and fight now for prayer in our churches, and that the house of God would be a house of prayer and that the children of God would be a people of prayer. Amen.

WHAT IS INTERCESSION?

The Biblical basis for intercession is described in Ezekiel 22:30-31. *"I looked for a man among them who would build up the wall and stand in the gap on behalf of the land so I would not have to destroy it, but I found none. So I will pour out my wrath on them and consume them with my fiery anger, bringing down on their heads all they have done, declares the Sovereign Lord."*

The picture painted here is that of God who has to judge the sin of the land. God sought for someone to intervene by acting as the defense lawyer, but there was none. Thus He was forced to pronounce a righteous judgment. In the heavenly realms Satan is the accuser (Job 1; Zechariah 3:1), and God is the judge. The intercessor stands in the gap on behalf of others to plead their case before the righteous judge of heaven and earth.

As believers we have been granted access into the throne room of the Father, and we may enter with boldness (Hebrews 10:19) in the name of Jesus. In this way, we stand in the gap and plead the case of those in need, and we ask that the blood of Jesus be applied to cover them and for grace to be extended to them.

The basic principle is explained in 2 Corinthians chapter 5. Paul addresses the issue of reconciliation and states, *"God reconciled us to Himself through Christ and then gave us the ministry of reconciliation."* This ministry of reconciliation includes our prayers on behalf of those who are in need of God's grace because of their sin. As we plead for them in the name of Christ our Intercessor (Hebrews 7:25), we act as legal defense to keep them from being judged. We are able to do this because Jesus paid the price and appointed us to this ministry. We face the accuser on behalf of others in the name of Jesus.

This means that intercession is the assignment of every believer. All of us are called to intercession. In the Old Testament the priests were the ones appointed to stand in the gap. In Numbers 16 the Israelites rebelled against Moses and Aaron. God responded by sending a plague. Moses sent Aaron with the censor into the midst of the people to stand in the gap and to make atonement for them. In the New Testament we are called to be priests under our eternal High Priest, Jesus. Every believer is called as a priest and to exercise the ministry of intercession and plead on behalf of others. We are all intercessors.

Those commonly called "intercessors" are people who spend more time in prayer than most believers and who enjoy doing this more than others. On this basis they are said to have the "gift of intercession."

There is no Biblical basis for this so-called "gift of intercession." Nowhere in Scripture is intercession ever described as a gift. Those who are commonly described as intercessors are believers that have a prophetic gift and as a result, enjoy spending time with God in prayer. They hear from God and speak to Him more than the average believer. Not all are prophets, but some are called to this office.

Some of us come from backgrounds where the prophetic gift is not recognized and thus not practiced. Even in circles where this gift is accepted as biblical, many tend to ignore it. The prophetic anointing often leads to unusual manifestations or actions, and often intercessors are therefore seen as "weird people." In fact, any study of the prophets will illustrate this perception. This can lead to fear and a lack of release to flow in this gift.

THE AUTHORITY OF THE INTERCESSOR

The authority for any intercession is based in the relationship with Jesus Christ, who is the main intercessor. *"Because Jesus lives forever, he has a permanent priesthood. Therefore he is able to save completely those who come to God through him, because he always lives to intercede for them."* (Hebrews 7:24-25).

In Christ, we have been made into a kingdom of priests (1 Peter 2:9). As royal priests we have the right and authority to intercede for individuals, cities and even nations. Jesus opened the way for us to enter into the presence of the Father, and we can enter into His presence anytime (Hebrews 10:19-22). In Christ we received the power to intercede for others and stand in the gap on their behalf against the enemy. This is a vital part of the ministry of reconciliation that God has given us (2 Corinthians 5:17-21), for it allows us the right to plead for others on the basis of the sacrifice of Christ.

In addition to opening the door to the Father, which allows us the privilege to intercede for others, the risen Lord has also given us authority and power to overcome the enemy. We are sent into the world by the very one who *"disarmed the powers and authorities and made a public spectacle of them, triumphing over them by the cross"* (Colossians 2:15). The risen Lord who was raised to the highest place and given a name that is above every name

(Philippians 2:9) has been given all authority in heaven and earth (Matthew 28:18). This risen Lord sent us, having been filled with the Holy Spirit, into the world with the authority and power to overcome the enemy (Mark 16:15-18; Acts 1:8).

Intercession is to move in the authority of Christ, entering into the presence of God to speak on behalf of those facing God's judgment and to oppose and overcome the enemy on their behalf through the power of the Holy Spirit. As the intercessor moves into the presence of God seeking His face on behalf of others, God reveals His will and plan for the specific situation. Once known, this perfect plan must be announced to the rulers and authorities in the heavenly realms to enforce God's will (Ephesians 3:11-12), but only when God gives the assignment and according to His timetable.

AUTHORITY RELEASED THROUGH THE CALL AND ASSIGNMENT

Not every intercessor moves in the same level of anointing and power. There are also levels of authority based on a person's call and assignment.

Jeremiah 1:5-10 relates the call of Jeremiah as prophet, and within this call there is a level of authority and power from God for this specific assignment. In the New Testament the apostle Paul received a mandate to preach to the Gentiles and with his call he received the authority and power for the work. In Acts 26:16-18 he recalls the moment he received his assignment in the following words: *"The Lord replied; 'Now get up and stand on your feet. I have appeared to you to appoint you as a servant and as a witness of what you have seen of me and what I will show you. I will rescue you from your own people and from the Gentiles. I am sending you to them to open their eyes and turn them from darkness to light and from the power of Satan to God, so that they might receive forgiveness of sins and a place among those who are sanctified by faith in me.'"*

This is a very important concept, because it limits the power of our intercession. When a person moves beyond the level of authority given in the specific assignment, it opens the door for the enemy, and many have paid a very high price by doing this. There is an interesting story in the book of Acts that illustrates this well. It is the story of the sons of Sceva, who used the names of Jesus and Paul, without knowing Jesus and without the anointing for the assignment (Acts 19:13-16). Note that the demon did not have to submit as they were moving outside of the authority, even though they used the name of Jesus!

RELATIONSHIP AND GEOGRAPHICAL LIMITS OF AUTHORITY

Levels of authority in intercession are determined by relationships and geographical scope. Parents have more authority than others to intercede for their children. In the same way, we have more authority to pray for our local community than for another community. This is why it is important to commit to our communities and families. The level of our commitment determines the authority to intercede effectively.

This important principle is taught in the portrayal of Jesus as the suffering servant in Isaiah 53:12. *"Therefore I will give Him a portion among the great and He will divide the spoils with the strong, because He poured out His life unto death and was numbered with the transgressors. For He bore the sin of many and made intercession for the transgressors."*

Note that even though He did not have to, Jesus chose to be numbered with the transgressors. He chose to be associated and counted among the transgressors. As a direct result of this choice, He received the authority and power to intercede for them. Our authority in intercession for people is directly dependent upon our willingness to associate with them.

The same principle applies to geographical areas. This is very clearly illustrated in the Book of Jeremiah. Most people readily quote Jeremiah 29:11-12, *"'For I know the plans I have for you,' declares the Lord, 'plans to prosper you and not to harm you, plans to give you a hope and a future. Then you will call upon me and come and pray to me and I will listen to you.'"* However, we rarely pay attention to the context of this passage! This is a letter from Jeremiah to the exiles in Babylon advising them to make a commitment to their city and community, in order that they may be blessed. It is very important to read Jeremiah 29:7 which states, *"Also seek the peace and prosperity of the city to which I have carried you into exile. Pray to the Lord for it, because if it prospers, you too will prosper."*

Our willingness to commit to people, cities, regions and nations directly determines the level of authority and corresponding power we have as intercessors. Where God sends you He gives you the power and authority to overcome, to succeed and to be victorious. He gave us all power and all authority. We are seated with Christ in heavenly places. He put everything under our feet. We don't need to be in fear but in faith.

SPHERES OF INFLUENCE

The above implies that we each have a specific sphere of influence in intercession. This sphere is primarily based on a person's specific call and assignment from God. It is also based on the level of commitment that the person makes to that call and assignment. This is reflected in the willingness of the person to commit to specific people and specific geographical boundaries.

This is not static and can increase through obedience and sacrifice. In 2 Corinthians 10:13-16, Paul touched on this concept. The church in Corinth was part of his assignment, and as they prospered and grew, he hoped that it would lead to an expansion of his ministry in the region. Paul was very clear that we have received the keys that are the power to bind and loose things on earth. However, we can only bind and loose what has all ready been bound or loosed in the heavenly realms. Moreover, we need the revelation from God to know what has been bound or loosed and whether or not it is our assignment and within our sphere of influence. This is to be done before we use the keys entrusted to us. Even experienced intercessors have moved outside of these parameters and paid a heavy price. This concept is particularly important when we deal with territorial spirits.

THE COVERING OF THE INTERCESSOR

Every intercessor should be part of a local church fellowship. We are all part of one body. This is a basic principle of Scripture. It is within the body of Christ, the Church, that we find the basis for our call and gifts (1 Corinthians 12:12-31).

Commitment to the local church is essential, no person can be detached from the body without loosing the connection to the head, Jesus Christ, from where all authority comes. In addition, every part of the body needs the other parts to function properly; Paul illustrated this in this passage. It is within the context of the local church that the empowering for ministry through gifts takes place. It is within this context that the vital elements of submission, obedience and accountability establish a protective covering for the intercessor.

THE DANGER OF THE LONE RANGER

The day of the Lone Ranger is long gone and I doubt highly if in fact it ever was the heart of God for His people. I believe His heart for His people and His Church is community and family. He doesn't want us to be dependent and He doesn't want us to be independent. He wants us to be interdependent, inter connected and interrelated. None of us is meant to be an island, but rightly connected and related to our brothers and sisters in the body of Christ.

In addition to the basic principle stated above, the act of intercession involves warfare, and any lone ranger puts themselves in a place of vulnerability without the protection of a covering body. In the Old Testament the soldiers were accompanied by armor bearers who fought alongside them (1 Samuel 14:1-14). Jesus sent his disciples out two by two. This basic principle applies to intercession as well as other aspects of ministry. Elijah failed immediately following a major victory, because he was alone and the enemy managed to discourage him (1 Kings 19).

The enemy seems to attack when people isolate themselves from the rest of the body of Christ. Similar to a wolf attacking a flock of sheep, they wait for one to stray then come between them and the flock and they become easy pickings. Some times he attacks our minds with the lie and if we don't have that voice of support we can fall into deception.

Another picture from Scripture illustrating this same principle of working and warring together and being there for one another is found in Exodus 17:8-13 which tells the story of the battle against the Amalekites. As Joshua fought the battle, Moses was on the mountain interceding, with his hands held up. As the battle raged, he became fatigued. Every time he dropped his hands, the enemy would be victorious. Aaron and Hur supported him by getting a stone for him to sit on while they held up his hands. Joshua and the troops won the battle because Moses was supported by these two men. Without this support, Moses would not have been able to maintain his position as intercessor.

The message is clear. Intercessors acting as lone rangers will pay a heavy price. In fact, most casualties in spiritual warfare come as a result of intercessors that move in presumption and without adequate support.

WHAT IS A COVERING?

The concept of spiritual covering and spiritual authority are principles not only in warfare but also in successful Christian living. It is closely related to the principles of covenant and the Lord is a covenant making and a covenant keeping God.

There have been misunderstandings, abuse and misuse in the area of spiritual authority and many of us in the body have been hurt and avoid the close relationships necessary for proper spiritual covering to be in place. One of the great benefits to the restoration of the five fold apostolic ministry is the understanding and birthing of relational networks that provide covering in the spirit of Sonship.

There are also many Pastors who are much more open to equipping activating and launching individuals into their area of ministry today. It comes down to learning to respect the giftings and callings in one another's life and partnering together in the harvest. Servant leadership and mentoring leadership is the covering model that Jesus and Paul demonstrated, rather than a covering from "over and above."

In the typical pastoral model this means going to your pastor and explaining the ministry and methods you intend to use and feel led to be involved in. Sharing your vision and the pastor coming along side of you and agreeing to stand with you and pray for you and walking together in a place of relationship and accountability. For this to function properly the parties need to be in agreement and the pastor or leader has to be able to speak into the vision and life of the individual in love and the individual needs to be open and teachable.

In the network model an individual normally needs to apply for membership and present their training and qualifications for ministry and then be credentialed or ordained by a governing body and overseen by an approved leader of that organization. The network model also many times works with and communicates with the individual's pastor. These groups also have ongoing training and fellowship opportunities to aid in the development and training of its associates.

At Eagle Worldwide Network of Ministries we have over 150 churches and ministries credentialed and we gather together a few times a year for growth days and have a support team in place to walk with and a prayer network to pray with the ongoing needs of our ministers.

MUTUAL ACCOUNTABILITY IS IMPORTANT

Mutual accountability is important but also misunderstood and at times this misunderstanding leaves us confused and hurt. I have to first and foremost understand spiritual authority and alignment before I can fully understand the need for and benefit of accountability. As a five fold leader in the body of Christ and one who serves in the role of Pastor at times and as a traveling itinerant minister other times and also an Apostolic overseer at other times, I get the unique opportunity to view the Body of Christ from different perspectives. Therefore, let me start by saying as I function and make decisions on a daily basis I can't please everyone nor can I be accountable to them on an individual basis. The Lord has brought people into my life and anointed and appointed them to speak into my life, people I trust and willfully submit myself to like Paul Wetzel my pastor, Dr. Jane Lowder, Apostle John Kelly, collectively the Board of Directors of Eagle Worldwide Ministries and certainly my wife Mave who I love and respect as my wife and also as a woman of God. I trust them and submit to them knowing that they will have my best interest in mind and will not purposefully violate that trust and will speak to me from a place of love and mutual respect.

When an individual joins our fellowship, one of the churches, or the Network of Ministries, we confirm that they are choosing to walk in submission to the authority established and ordained of God as the leadership of that work. The deeper the level of commitment and covenant relationship we have will usually indicate the level of authority and responsibility. I have to interact in that relationship and many times I've found that correction without love and proper relationship breeds rebellion.

I've found in my own personal life that walking under proper covering and authority brought with it a greater level of power and feelings of protection and security.

There is also a peer level of accountability where to a certain degree, I am by relationship and respect open to the opinions of others I am working with like my leadership team or co workers on projects etc., but that's not a place of spiritual accountability but rather a place of a working relationship. I want to be the best I can be for the Lord as well as for myself and family, so I try to be as open and teachable as possible. I believe when you're green you're growing and when you're ripe you're rotten when you think you know everything you really don't know anything; that education is an on-going, life-long process that occurs much more though relationship, experience, personal interaction, and trial and error than it ever does though the typical academic outlets. I hope this gives you a better understand of walking in mutual accountability and under spiritual authority. There are two books on this subject that I have benefited from and would recommend you read; one is by John Bevere called Undercover and the other is by Watchmen Neie called Spiritual Authority.

There is a growing need for this kind of mutual accountability in the church. On the one hand, pastors and leaders are to protect the intercessors. They need to learn how to release and free them to do their ministry without hindrance and without controlling their ministry. This can only happen through building relationships and respecting the prophetic ministry of the intercessors, even when they share some words of correction. This is illustrated in the Old Testament where the prophets had access to the court of the king. The kings that allowed the prophets access and accepted their words were blessed. The most powerful example is David accepting the severe rebuke of Nathan the prophet.

We have found tremendous hurt among intercessors as we work with them. The vast majority of intercessors have been hurt, often very severely, by those in leadership in churches. Many pastors are like King Ahab in the story recorded in 1 Kings 22. He did not want to ask the prophet Micah's opinion, for he hated him, because "he never prophesies anything good about me." In fact, the label "intercessor" is often used by leaders as a way to control the prophetic anointing.

Intercessors in turn need to learn how to handle the information they receive from God. Most of the words given to intercessors are for the prayer closet and not for public proclamation.

Much of the damage done in churches is the direct result of a lack of relationship and accountability between leaders and intercessors.

THE DIFFERENT KINDS OF INTERCESSORS

UNIQUE AND ONE OF A KIND

Not all intercessors are alike in their callings, their personalities, their assignments and their styles of prayer. God has made every one unique in every way.

PERSONALITY

Every one of us has a different personality given by God. We are unique creatures and no two will respond in exactly the same way to different situations. There are largely four kinds of personalities, and we tend to be a blend of these, with one being dominant. One way to depict this is by using the prophetic picture of the creatures in Ezekiel. Each creature had the following four faces: the face of a man, the face of a lion, the face of an ox, and the face of an eagle.

- The face of a man is the personality of an extrovert. This person receives energy from interaction with people and enjoys the company of others. In terms of intercession they enjoy praying with and for people and their needs.

- The face of the lion is the dominant personality. This is the person who can and will take charge and will move with authority. This person prays with authority and boldness and enjoys spiritual warfare.

- The face of the ox is the personality of the person who will faithfully persevere. This person will carry a load and keep on working. In intercession this person will faithfully pray over lists, preparing the ground for the harvest, even if he does not see immediate results.

- The face of the eagle is the personality of the person who is able to soar up into the presence of God and enjoys intimacy with God above all else. This person will often see in the spiritual realm and sense things that others miss. They often are the seers or watchmen, sensing danger or announcing future events.

ASSIGNMENTS

Many intercessors are called for a specific assignment:

- Some are called to pray for individuals. They will faithfully cover the needs of those individuals.
- Sometimes it is individuals they are related to or come in contact with on a regular basis and at times it's individuals the Holy Spirit lays on their heart in a flash or a moment. Sometimes it is a person of prominence such as an athlete or entertainer. Other times, a person who seems unrelated in any way but the intercessor feels that gentle and familiar urging of the Spirit.
- At times this can occur rather suddenly and at other times it is something that becomes a burden over time. The intercessor becomes more and more sensitive to these promptings: how to start, when that burden lifts, and how to finish. The object is to learn to be led by the Spirit.
- One of the most important areas of intercession is the covering of leaders by committed intercessors. Spiritual leaders need prayer covering because they are objects of attack by the enemy, targets because he knows if he attacks and defeats the head it affects the body. Both pastor and flock are affected.
- Some intercede for specific causes. Some pray with unusual intensity for issues like abortion or the homeless, carrying this burden in prayer into the throne room time and time again or Christian education or pending political legislation, etc.
- Some intercessors have a special assignment with authority for specific groups of people. The apostle Paul had a specific call and authority to reach the Gentiles. In the same way, intercessors can have specific assignments for people groups such as

ethnic groups like aboriginals or other minorities that have been or are being persecuted.
- Others are called to intercede for cities, regions, or nations. In recent years, many have prayer walked streets of their city or region. Others have traveled to specific regions or nations to complete prayer assignments. There is specific power and authority released as we step out in faith and literally put our feet down to claim the territory assigned to us.

STYLES OF PRAYER

Intercessors pray differently. In Scripture there are different kinds of prayer. In 1 Timothy 2 Paul writes that God wants all men everywhere to be saved and therefore that all kinds of prayer be made by all. In this passage he mentions four different kinds of prayer.

- Requests: This is the kind of prayer in which the intercessor brings specific needs to God, particularly on behalf of others.
- Prayers: This is the most common Greek word for prayer in the New Testament and is used with a descriptive word. It is always tied to a specific action that accompanies it. Thus we read about prayer and fasting, prayer and giving, etc.
- Intercession: This is the kind of prayer where we stand in "the place of meeting" to meet the enemy and overcome him on behalf of someone else.
- Thanksgiving: This is the kind of prayer that breaks open the heavens and brings the unexpected.

PUTTING IT ALL TOGETHER

The key is to know your calling and to learn to pray accordingly. Usually each person has a blend of calling, personality, gifting, and style of prayer. Thus the lion personality will often have a warrior anointing and pray in the style of intercession. The eagle personality will often be a seer and function as a watchman. We each tend to pray according to the unique person that God made each one of us to be.

At the same time one needs to be careful not to fall into a rut, but to stretch in the areas of weakness. God will at times put us in a position where we are stretched beyond our comfort zone. In personality and prayer our example is comfort zone. In personality and prayer our example is Jesus who was balanced as a person and was able to meet the needs of all people.

We must keep in mind we are not the burden bearer, but the Lord. It is our job is to carry it to Him. In faith, to leave it at his feet, and go and carry the next assignment, and the next. I talk to Intercessors who always seem to be worn out and tired and say they don't understand their burden, but I do, and I know that its' not the Lord's intent, He gives us joy and peace even in the midst of our battles and struggles. I have to remember that the battle belongs to the Lord, and maintain the proper balances and safeguards in my life to ensure my well-being and guard against fatigue by using wisdom and understanding.

Corporate prayer is a great place to be stretched, for in corporate prayer the different kinds of personalities, gifts and callings are brought together and joined in unity. When praying corporately, there needs to be a yielding to the Spirit to allow for these kinds of prayer and personalities. When this happens a powerful anointing is released and the atmosphere for miracles is created.

THE NEED FOR CORPORATE INTERCESSION

Although many intercessors spend long hours in personal prayer closets, there is a very real need and place for corporate intercession. In Matthew 18:18-20 Jesus said:

"I tell you the truth, whatever you bind on earth will have been bound in heaven and whatever you loose on earth will have been loosed in heaven. Again, I tell you that if two of you on earth agree about anything you ask for, it will be done for you by My Father in heaven. For where two or three come together in My name, there I am with them."

THE POWER AND AUTHORITY OF CORPORATE INTERCESSION

There is a specific power and authority released when believers come together in prayer in the name of Jesus. The risen Lord manifests His presence and releases His power though the Holy Spirit. This picture can best be understood in light of Ephesians 2, which speaks of our salvation by grace. Included in this grace is the fact that *"God raised us up with Christ and seated us with him in heavenly places in Christ Jesus"* (Ephesians 2:6). When we come together corporately, we become the very instrument created by God to do the work that he called us as a church body to do (Ephesians 2:10). The key to this is the unity we have in Christ, beginning with the racial unity between Jew and Gentile.

As we move into corporate intercession, we step into the presence of the Father where Jesus is seated in the place of authority. He manifests Himself as head of the body, and we receive the revelation of God's will and the "kairos" time for His will. We get to know the mysteries of God, as Paul came to know the mystery that the Gentiles were heirs with Israel through the Gospel (Ephesians 3:1-6). Once he understands this mystery, his call as apostle to the Gentiles became clear, and he moved with divine authority to set captives free. As we move in corporate intercession, God reveals to us what is bound and what is loosed in heaven. Thus our prayers are able to line up with God's will and time *"to declare the manifold wisdom of God to the rulers and authorities in the heavenly realms, according to His eternal will which He accomplished in Christ Jesus"* (Ephesians 3:10-11). It is as we declare the will of God to these powers that we are able to enforce this will on earth by binding and loosing what has been bound and loosed in heaven.

Corporate intercession is the key to release the power to overcome the enemy. Our battle is *"not against flesh and blood, but against the rulers and authorities and powers of this dark world and against the spiritual forces of evil in the heavenly realms"* (Ephesians 6:12). These rulers and authorities are the same ones mentioned in Ephesians 3:10-11. Now the next verse underlines the fact that we are dealing with corporate intercession as we do this: "In Him (i.e. Jesus) and through faith in Him we (*plural*) may approach God with freedom and confidence." This is further underscored by the prayer that Paul prays in Ephesians 3:14-21. It is in Christ that we receive the inner strength and confidence we need for the battle and the key to power is as we discover together with the saints what the true extent of the love of Christ encompasses. It is in this relationship with other believers that we are filled to the measure of the fullness of God (Ephesians 3:18-19). Once we grasp this, He is able to do immeasurably more than we can ever ask or imagine (Ephesians 3:20-21).

With that Paul moves to the key issue of unity in Ephesians 4:1-6. The unity of the body in the Spirit is the key to releasing the power necessary to enforce the will of God on earth in the face of the enemy. Jesus said that it is the unity of the church that will cause the world to believe in Him (John 17:20-21). That unity proves to the world that God sent His Son and loves them even as He has loved Jesus (John 17:22-23). In corporate intercession, we move into the presence of God in the heavenly realms and reflect the glory of God in ever increasing ways (2 Corinthians 3:18). At the same time we move into the realm of the Spirit and become empowered with divine weapons to pull down strongholds. We demolish arguments and every pretension that sets itself up against the knowledge of God, and we take captive every thought and make it obedient to Christ (2 Corinthians 10:4-5).

The whole idea of incremental increase in power through unity is found in the Old Testament. This can be seen in Leviticus 26:8, *"Five of you shall chase a hundred, and a hundred of you shall put ten thousand to flight; your enemies shall fall by the sword before you."* As we come together in unity and seek God's word for a specific situation, we overcome the demonic forces as we pronounce the Word of God for the specific situation. The prophetic proclamation through corporate intercession is the most powerful weapon we have and can break through the opposition of the powers of hell. In fact, corporate intercession brings revelation from the Spirit that becomes the key to bind and loose. Even the gates of hell can't stand against this (Matthew 16:17-19).

SOME PRACTICAL ISSUES

- Leadership: This is very important, particularly when there is a large gathering. Leaders are necessary to ensure the unity of the gathering and must be sensitive to the different personalities, giftings, and styles of prayer so that these blend together in harmony under the direction of the Spirit. The leader must have administrative gifts, as well as the gift of discernment. It is crucial that the leader ensure that no flaky intercession takes place. Most importantly, the leader has to be sensitive to the guidance of the Spirit and lead accordingly, so that all move in unity in the direction of the Spirit's guidance.

- Warfare: When a group gets involved in major warfare, strong leadership is absolutely essential. In this area it is preferable to work with mature intercessors. It may be necessary to restrict it to people who know each other so that the unity is not compromised in any way.

- Training: Corporate intercession provides a wonderful setting to train and develop the prophetic gift. The key is to have it properly structured with strong yet sensitive oversight. Often the variety of the prophetic gifts flowing together provides the opportunity for the mature intercessors to model the prophetic gift to others. As they lead intercession, they are able to sense and encourage the gifts in the less mature intercessors through recognizing strengths and weaknesses and providing encouragement and advice.
- Accountability: Corporate intercession without accountability leads to many problems. Confidentiality and accountability are essential. One major pitfall is that it can become a center and source of gossip. This is why corporate intercession demands quality leaders who are accountable to local leadership. Corporate intercession is the most powerful weapon we can use against the enemy, but it is neglected by many. It is time to move forward and employ the full arsenal of divine weapons.

GUIDELINES FOR SELECTING A TEAM

Let's talk about selecting an intercessory prayer team. Let me start by saying, not every prayer warrior will make a good intercessor. The following are some of the things I most often look for in an intercessor.

I set up the following guidelines and have used them to establish intercessory prayer groups. You may find them to be a little strict, but I have found, particularly at the beginning, that if I set my sights and expectations high for individuals, then they rise to the occasion. I have also found that its easier to let the reins out than it is to pull them in. I have found that a degree of structure can bear fruit, not just in the area of intercession, but in other areas of the team members' lives. By the way, more than anything else, I am looking for a walk of holiness, as we strive for excellence in ministry, and excellence is the best you can do.

1. Are they well rooted in their Christian walk? (I'm looking for people who are balanced in spirit, word and action.) Because intercession is an end time ministry that involves spiritual warfare, it is important that those who participate are walking in obedience to God in His word and are walking under the covering of God given authority such as their pastor etc. Ultimately, attacks will come so they must not have any open doors in their life and walk.

2. I am looking for people who have an intimate relationship with God. Usually they reveal that in ordinary, daily conversation. Knowing God is the foundation of communication.

3. I want to know that they have a personal prayer life. Intercession should not take the place of personal prayer time, for, when we come to the place of intercession, we are coming to minister unto God. Intercession is NOT my prayer time; it is my ministry call and work.

4. I am looking for those who can walk in unity as a team player. I am certainly not looking for a lone ranger, nor for a person who brings attention to themselves; for it is getting lost in the heart of God, in that place of humility, that brings forth the fruit of intercession.

5. I am looking for a person who is dependable. I'm talking here in a practical sense. If people bounce in and out of the team, and in and out of the meetings, they could become more of a distraction despite having many spiritual gifts.

THINGS TO ASK WHEN SELECTING A TEAM

1. Can they make most of the meetings?

2. Do they show up on time?

3. Is their walk up and down, or can I depend on the fact that next week, month or even next year they will still be serving the Lord. I am looking for people who at every turn are not requiring or are in constant need of personal ministry because when we come together as a team we need to be ministers. None of us are perfect. We all need ministry from time to time, but if your team is in constant need of ministry you'll not get the work done that God has called you to do. Spiritual maturity and dependability are very important.

Finally, I am looking for people baptized in the Holy Spirit with an evidence of some gifting, particularly in the areas of prophecy and the revelatory gifts. When we are making the selections we need to be led by the Holy Spirit, by praying to see who is called to the team. Didn't Jesus pray, as He selected His disciples? I think it is critical that we pray over all the applicants and select them according to merit, gifting and most importantly, the prompting of the Spirit of God.

HOW DOES CORPORATE INTERCESSION WORK?

As you can probably tell by now, I like prayer. I like it to flow freely, and I feel the most effective meetings are those that are free to flow as the Spirit of God leads. I also see great benefit in some order and structure, so the following is a guide to how I would hold a typical meeting. Before beginning I would like to say that the Lord always finds it rather easy to interrupt my meetings... HALLELUJAH!!! It is important even when you are praying before a meeting that you let Holy Spirit know He can move any way He wants.

A PRACTICAL PROTOCOL:

1. Take a few minutes and examine your hearts for you are preparing to mount the hill of God as it says in Psalms 24:3-6. *"Who may ascend into the hill of the Lord? Or who may stand in His holy place? He who has clean hands and a pure heart, who has not lifted up his soul to an idol nor sworn deceitfully, He shall receive blessings from the Lord and righteousness from the God of his salvation. This is Jacob, the generation of those who seek Him, who seek your face."*

2. Place a small container on the altar or in front of the meeting room with paper and pens. Allow each participant an opportunity to write down anything they are praying for personally or any issue that could pose as a distraction as they attempt to enter into intercession. Rip them up before the Lord and dispose of them in the box, while praying and asking Him to remove any distraction or burden so that during this time of intercession everyone can focus fully on ministering to Him, allowing each person an opportunity to see, hear, and feel the voice of God, and for the desires of His heart to be made known. The object of intercession is not to pray our own desire, thoughts, or what we logically figure out in our own minds, but instead to seek His face, His heart and His desires.

3. Put on worship music, begin to praise and worship freely, any way or style you desire. Dance, sing, laugh, cry, stand or kneel, however you feel to honour your King. No one should leave the room, but everyone should worship God and allow Him to lead and speak to them individually.

During this period, another leader and I would go around and anoint with oil all of the intercessors, asking God to increase the anointing for intercession and prophecy and to release the prophetic anointing into the meeting and individuals. I anoint them that they might receive revelation, wisdom and understanding, which are the hallmarks to knowing what God wants us to minister in prayer.

Revelation is what we see, hear or feel in our spirit.

Understanding is the interpretation of what that revelation means. One revelation may have two or three correct interpretations, or just one. Many times when we interpret the revelation we get insight and understanding on how that revelation can apply to our own personal lives and also to the church or to a certain group in the city, religion, nation or church at large.

Wisdom is knowing what to do with the revelation. Do we pray it, act it out, speak it, proclaim it, or walk it out? Many times the prayer we pray back to the Father can be in proclamation or in a prophetic action like the Jericho Prayer Walk.

After praying for a while the leader will call all the people together. You can all stand in a circle and share the revelation received during the prayer time. This revelation is what we believe the Lord wants us to pray. Each person should get an opportunity to share what the Lord has laid on their hearts. Share quickly, don't ramble or preach a sermon. Get right to the point and say what He said and what you saw. Then you should go around the circle again and pray it all in, quickly and precisely. It is not the length of the prayer, it is the spirit of the prayer and that we prayed the prayer He told us to pray. When you have completed the prayer, one of the leaders should pray a covering prayer and a prayer of unity over all the intercessors. At that point, the meeting ends, but I normally stay a while to provide personal prayer ministry to any who need or desire personal ministry at that time.

CLOSING PRAYER

Heavenly Father, I come to You in the name of Jesus Christ and in the power of the Holy Spirit and I ask You, Master, to anoint my brothers and sisters and these words, that they might receive a fresh anointing, a fresh empowerment in their lives. I ask You, Father, to anoint their prayer lives, to light up their prayer closets. Let their times of prayer and intimacy with You be the most exciting moments of their lives. I ask You, Father, to impart and increase the anointing for intercession on every person who reads this book. I ask You to give them revelation from the heavenlies. I ask You, Master, to break their hearts, with the things that break Your heart. Let their hearts cry when Your heart cries, let their hearts laugh when Your heart laughs. Let their heart sing when Your heart sings. I ask you, Master, to give them a burden for the poor and the broken, for the weak and for the lost. I ask You Lord to let them soar into heavenly places, to let them soar in the Spirit, walk in the Spirit and live in the Spirit every day. I ask You to bless them and that everywhere they go and everything they do, that all that see them will see Jesus in them. In Jesus' name. Amen.

CHAPTER 8

END TIME SPIRITS

I believe that there are five end time spirits that are opposing the church of Jesus Christ today in a very real and direct way. These are the five ruler spirits that are directly opposing us today like never before.

In Ephesians 6:10-18 Paul describes the warfare mandate on the emerging end time church.

"[10]Finally, my brethren, be strong in the Lord and in the power of His might. [11]Put on the whole armor of God, that you may be able to stand against the wiles of the devil. [12]For we do not wrestle against flesh and blood, but against principalities, against powers, against the rulers of the darkness of this age, against spiritual hosts of wickedness in the heavenly places. [13]Therefore take up the whole armor of God, that you may be able to withstand in the evil day, and having done all, to stand. [14]Stand therefore, having girded your waist with truth, having put on the breastplate of righteousness, [15]and having shod your feet with the preparation of the gospel of peace; [16]above all, taking the shield of faith with which you will be able to quench all the fiery darts of the wicked one. [17]And take the helmet of salvation, and the sword of the Spirit, which is the word of God; [18]praying always with all prayer and supplication in the Spirit, being watchful to this end with all perseverance and supplication for all the saints."

Paul describes the warfare mandate on the emerging end time church. He talks about putting on the whole armour of God to stand against the strategies of the enemy, telling us our battle and fight is not in the natural, but in the Spirit. He also talks about our responsibility in protecting ourselves and those around us and fighting back in prayer for the victory. In verse 12, He talks about those different levels of spiritual authority and power that are in the world today.

These five spirits I believe are at the root of most of the problems we experience today in the church.

- The spirit of Religion
- The spirit of Witchcraft
- The spirit of Leviathan
- The spirit of Offense
- The spirit of Jezebel

1. THE SPIRIT OF RELIGION

The spirit of religion, I believe, is the spirit that opposing the move of God in our lives individually and collectively in this end time season more than any other spirit.

The Israelites were waiting for Messiah when the first disciples recognized that Jesus, Yeshua, was the Messiah. They had trouble equating in their own mind because they thought that Christ came to set them free from the Roman Empire and the natural bondage they were in. Actually, His primary purpose was to set them free from the spiritual bondage of religion that was put upon them by the Pharisees and the religious community of their day.

C. Peter Wagner and his wife Doris, who are true pioneers in deliverance and spiritual warfare in our generation, talk about the power and purpose of this religious spirit and how it operates against us in their book, "Free From the Religious Spirit."

They founded the International Society of Deliverance Ministries, of which I am a member. They have since turned this organization over to Bill and Janet Sudduth, as the largest group of deliverance ministers recognized in the world.

The Bible tells us that our religion and our tradition in Mark 7:13 can bring the Word of God to no effect. The religious spirit will block my ability to bring life to the written Word through the power of the Spirit, and will try to bring me to account for the letter of the law, by way of condemnation rather than spiritual conviction.

Also, I can recognize that spirit operating in my life when I become critical and judgmental concerning other people in the Christian community, and even try to use the Word to correct and condemn people I am in relationship with.

The third way I recognize this spirit operating against me is when I broadly look at the community and see that they have an appearance of godliness yet deny the power thereof. Paul describes this in 2 Timothy 3 in his dialogue concerning the end time church in verse 5. He talks about this religious experience having the form of godliness but denying the power, from such people turn away. He describes it again in verse 7 where he says these people are ever learning and never able to come to the knowledge of God through the truth.

2. THE SPIRIT OF WITCHCRAFT

There are four types of basic witchcraft.

THE OCCULT

One type of witchcraft is the occult, which is actually rather easy to recognize and is described in Deuteronomy 18:9-14 *"[9]When you come into the land which the LORD your God is giving you, you shall not learn to follow the abominations of those nations. [10]There shall not be found among you anyone who makes his son or his daughter pass through the fire, or one who practices witchcraft, or a soothsayer, or one who interprets omens, or a sorcerer, [11]or one who conjures spells, or a medium, or a spiritist, or one who calls up the dead. [12]For all who do these things are an abomination to the LORD, and because of these abominations the LORD your God drives them out from before you. [13]You shall be blameless before the LORD your God. [14]For these nations which you will dispossess listened to soothsayers and diviners; but as for you, the LORD your God has not appointed such for you."*

Below is a list the Word of God talks about and what they mean:

- Divination (fortune teller)
- Observer or times (soothsayer)
- Prediction (psychic)
- Enchanter (magician)
- Witch (sorcerer)
- Charmer (hypnotist)
- Familiar Spirits (Medium/spirit guide)
- Wizard (a clairvoyant – psychic)
- Necromancer (consults the dead – like a medium)

In Leviticus 19:30 He is talking about seeking after wizards which is a clairvoyant or psychic and in Leviticus 20:6 *"And the person who turns to mediums and familiar spirits, to prostitute himself with them, I will set My face against that person and cut him off from his people."* The Lord says He will cut off His people, those who go whoring after witchcraft.

Our enemy can also be rather subtle and seductive. Many of these practices are well accepted today in the mainstream parts of our society and are highlighted and embellished in all forms of contemporary media. God tells me to guard my heart. I need to make sure I don't open the door of my heart, which leads to a slippery slope of giving witchcraft a stronghold and Satan the authority to operate in my life.

ROOT OF REBELLION/ANARCHY: ANTI-SUBMISSION

1 Samuel 15:23 *"For rebellion is as the sin of witchcraft, and stubbornness is iniquity and idolatry. Because you have rejected the word of the LORD, He also has rejected you from being king."*

The root of rebellion was the sin of witchcraft. It was rebellion that caused Saul his kingdom, and his promise. Today as never before, we can see rebellion at work in our society, and if we look more closely, in most of our own lives as well. I have struggled many years with rebellion in my own life, starting with rules and authority against my parents, which was carried over into my education and adult life.

By the grace of God it was revealed to me that we all need to be aware of it. It usually starts off with anti-submission, independence, then into rebellion and finally anarchy and chaos.

If you haven't already noticed, you can look at the news any and every day and realize that it is one of the spirits that is at work right now in our society. Without divine intervention and personal accountability there is anarchy and rebellion that leads to violence that we are seeing on the international news everyday. It has permeated through every thread of our society.

MANIPULATION AND CONTROL

Under manipulation and control, are witchcraft spirits such as Jezebel spirits of domination, abuse, and seduction.

Even in our advertising and basic governmental structures we can see the enemy releasing witchcraft to control our lives even to the point of what we purchase, how we dress, and other acceptable and unacceptable aspects of our life style. If these spirits were not powerful and didn't work effectively against us, then automobile manufacturers would be hiring the best engineers and mechanics to advertise their products as opposed to sexually seductive male and female models.

The image of the Marlboro man and the whole seductive concept causes many people to begin to smoke and ultimately die of cancer, so the devil's plan and purpose is fulfilled — to steal, kill and destroy.

Nike, Levis, Gucci and other brand names would certainly be a lot less expensive and a lot less desirable but for these powerful spirits.

CHARISMATIC WITCHCRAFT

Charismatic Witchcraft is a very dangerous form of witchcraft that operates in the church and in other ministries and Christian forums. I've seen situations where it operates in one Christian against another, a husband against his wife, the Pastor against his people and vice versa. It occurs when people use the Word of God or their spiritual gifts, authority or power to manipulate or control another person or situations contrary to the will and purposes of God.

I've seen leaders use their position and authority to keep people in their church or ministry and also people use their gifts in an ungodly way to gain a position or exert their influence over a Pastor or leader.

I've been in counseling sessions where I've seen husbands and wives use the word of God to attack their spouse or a loved one and get them to do what they want. I've heard people pray witchcraft prayers toward other people and even at times, trying to manipulate God. We all need to be careful to pray for God's will to be done in one another's life and to use and not abuse the power, authority and influence He's given us for His plan and purposes to be fulfilled and not our own.

3. THE SPIRIT OF LEVIATHAN

We see in Job 41:1-9,

"¹Can you pull in Leviathan with a fishhook or tie down its tongue with a rope? ²Can you put a cord through its nose or pierce its jaw with a hook? ³Will it keep begging you for mercy? Will it speak to you with gentle words? ⁴Will it make an agreement with you for you to take it as your slave for life? ⁵Can you make a pet of it like a bird or put it on a leash for the young women in your house? ⁶Will traders barter for it? Will they divide it up among the merchants? Can you fill its hide with harpoons or its head with fishing spears? ⁸If you lay a hand on it, you will remember the struggle and never do it again! ⁹Any hope of subduing it is false; the mere sight of it is overpowering."

Leviathan is a powerful spirit referenced in Job 41. One of his chief jobs is to block deliverance. It is a ruler demon over our continent of North America and there are many other spirits interconnected with it. The root spirits of rebellion, worldliness and festive activities, loving the things of this world and the spirit of mammon and the spirit of entertainment are all part of the root spirits that are rooted in the Spirit of Leviathan. I believe he is the ruler demon over Las Vegas and New Orleans.

Isaiah 27:1 *"In that day, the LORD will punish with his sword — his fierce, great and powerful sword — Leviathan the gliding serpent, Leviathan the coiling serpent; he will slay the monster of the sea."*

The book of Isaiah is like a mini gospel, the truth of Christ. His birth, his life, his message, even his death are all prophesied by Isaiah years before it happened.

I say to you in this time and season, when the new wine is being poured out around the world, you are going to begin to see the power of God slay the serpent that is Leviathan.

First, it has to be exposed, and is being exposed right now around the world. There were years where people never heard anything about Leviathan and didn't even know what it was. Now there is great teaching coming forth and revealing how it operates because Jesus is going to deal with that spirit. He talks about how he is going to go and put a hook in the snoot of that serpent Leviathan and pull it out. He is going to pull it out of the body of the church. I tell you, He is not going to deal nicely with this spirit. When you look at Leviathan, it is pictured in many books as a snake or crocodile because of its ancient history, back to Egyptian roots and even into eastern cultures. In 1 Corinthians 6:9 we see, *"Or do you not know that wrongdoers will not inherit the kingdom of God? Do not be deceived: Neither the sexually immoral nor idolaters nor adulterers nor men who have sex with men"*

Verse 17 says *"But whoever is united with the Lord is one with him in spirit."*

He is talking about our own body being the temple of the Holy Ghost. One of the ploys of Leviathan in this season is attacking not just the Body of Christ, but also our families, our children and us.

Once your lifestyle is under the blood and you have confessed and repented, He no longer sees that sin. He said when I confess my sin He is faithful and true to cleanse me from all unrighteousness. So I do not want to fall under condemnation. We are part of the One New Man.

Take a good look at the spirits fighting over our families. Leviathan is a worldly spirit and a festive spirit like Mardi Gras. Addictions are a huge part of how that spirit is operating against our children. Addictions and addictive spirits are opposing our children at a very young age. Spirits of entertainment are opening up our children to spiritual attack through TV, Movies, radio, music, video games etc. Every which way, our people are under attack.

This generation has been marked with an X by the enemy and said they will never be any good. But God has His heart set on this generation and He is going to bring restoration. This is the generation that is going to call in the Glory of the Lord and seek His face. This generation is going to take the land.

We need to remember that God loves the sinner but hates the sin. His love makes the difference. Speak truth and life. A sword in one hand and a towel in the other. That's the way to wage spiritual warfare. The sword of the Spirit which is the Word of God to fight and defeat the enemy and a towel to wash our brother's and sister's feet with love, to forgive, encourage and strengthen them.

This worldly spirit is attacking us on every front. You can't avoid going into the world. There is going to be times when you have to go to the forefront. It is the heart of God for us to learn how to fight and how to do battle.

Drugs and addiction, right now, are the spirits causing us to defile our own bodies, even as children.

My desire for success took me over the edge. You have got to remember that money is not evil but the love of money, the enterprise and success, the worshipping of those things and where you place them in your life; that's the root of evil. You need to make the most important thing the most important thing and put it in priority order. He wants us to prosper and be victorious.

One of the problems of why these spirits are so successful against this younger generation is because we have not let the true love and light of Jesus Christ shine in the church. There is a hunger in every man and woman's heart for God. There is a void and only God can fill it. That yearning in our young people is what has caused them to go over to the other side.

We need to bring the prophetic to the world, but we have been shut down by religion and made to quiet the very message and hope of God.

Addictions are rooted in the Spirit of Leviathan. Methamphetamine, crack cocaine and the mixture of certain chemicals that are used on their own would definitely kill you, but combined in a certain mixture make people do things they would never do. Methadone is one of the end time methods rooted in sorcery. Users, dealers, sorcery, domination, the occult, divination and witchcraft, manipulation and control; these are all the powers trying to rob us of our destiny, calling and anointing. We need to separate ourselves from the consumption of worldly things. Don't get me wrong; I am for success according to the Biblical principles of God, however, success with integrity. Spirits of Leviathan are covenant-breaking spirits. It causes problems with Bible study, with concentrating on spiritual goals. I have to have spiritual goals. There is a greater reason why I was birthed and rebirthed. What is my greater purpose? Why was I born for such a time as this? What part am I going to play? You have to sit down and develop goals, for you and your family.

God wants us to be impactful, to have attainable goals and objectives. You need to take your energy, your effort, and your finances and sow them back. Leviathan causes problems in your concentrating on spiritual goals.

The Bible tells us that in the last days men will become lovers of pleasure. We need to do the work of ministry. That spirit puts fear in our heart and tries to distract us.

Learning problems such as ADD are a spiritual disease, many times, generational. Leviathan's ultimate goal is mind control, mood altering, depression, distraction and confusion. Many people have been set free in deliverance from this.

Another manifestation is hardness of heart and cold heartedness, making it so people cannot feel. The root of hard heartedness is the spirit of Leviathan. When one is under that spirit they cannot give or receive love properly and it is usually rooted in some form of condemnation against themselves. We need to be the lifter of those around us.

4. THE SPIRIT OF JEZEBEL

Jezebel has no gender and comes against spiritual authority. She misrepresents the prophets of the Lord. In 1 Kings 21:8 *"So she wrote letters in Ahab's name, placed his seal on them, and sent them to the elders and nobles who lived in Naboth's city with him."*

Jezebel attacks the prophetic church and ministries and the office of the prophet and also tries to keep the people from hearing the voice of the Lord.

1 Kings 18:19 *"Now summon the people from all over Israel to meet me on Mount Carmel. And bring the four hundred and fifty prophets of Baal and the four hundred prophets of Asherah, who eat at Jezebel's table."* Jezebel had her own prophets. She had 450 prophets of Baal. They sat at her table and prophesied what she wanted to hear. Jezebel cannot operate without an Ahab who gives up his God given place of authority. When under the influence of Jezebel the people involved believe they have been highly favoured of God for some spiritually high place for God and conclude they have some divine secret strength. Eventually, they become unteachable and uncorrectable. They continually try to arrange private meetings and alliances. They begin to show sour fruit and you begin to see patterns of broken relationships, lone rangers and in the end, they do not usually remain under someone's covering. They are critical towards leadership and the vision of the group. Hebrews 12:14-16 says, *"Make every effort to live in peace with everyone and to be holy; without holiness no one will see the Lord. [15] See to it that no one falls short of the grace*

of God and that no bitter root grows up to cause trouble and defile many. [16] See that no one is sexually immoral, or is godless like Esau, who for a single meal sold his inheritance rights as the oldest son."

A Jezebel spirit sows seeds of discord — 1 Kings 21:25 says *"There was never anyone like Ahab, who sold himself to do evil in the eyes of the LORD, urged on by Jezebel his wife."* The Word of God warns us to not tolerate this spirit. Revelation 2:20, *"Nevertheless, I have this against you: You tolerate that woman Jezebel, who calls herself a prophet. By her teaching she misleads my servants into sexual immorality and the eating of food sacrificed to idols."* In Revelation 2:28 we will have the favour of God to overcome, *"I will also give that one the morning star."*

5. THE SPIRIT OF OFFENSE

If I am easily offended and continually offended and am hurt and broken and I constantly go back in to that area again, when I go back I open that door again.

If I feel offended and leave that door open, that spirit is going to try and ravage me. Its' objective is to try to bring me back. How often? Every time I allow myself to be offended. Every time I allow myself to harbor unforgiveness I have to repent. I have to repent to God for my behavior and repent to the person who offended me. That is why the Word says if I have a problem with my brother, I've got to go and see my brother, then go to the altar. So now I have the process of staying free.

We have to resist the devil and the devil will flee. If I give place to the devil and continue by allowing those same spirits and feelings to continue, then the same behavior patterns will control me.

The battlefield is in your mind. The spirit of offense is an end time enemy. There are a very high percentage of people under the influence of offense. Consequently, they cannot maintain and stand in their spiritual position. Sometimes when God is trying to bless us, maybe with a prophetic word, maybe with a hug, or an embrace from somebody who says "Hey, I love you", we are offended and our mind drifts to this person who offended us. Instead of being able to receive the blessing from that person or anyone else, I am thinking about how they hurt me.

The preacher is preaching, separating the Word, the Holy Spirit is trying to speak to me, but because I am offended, my mind is thinking, 'I wonder why Sister Suzie or Brother Bob didn't talk to me. I wonder if they don't like me any more. I wonder if I said something to them last week. I wonder if they think I'm this or that. I wonder if they are all talking about me. They probably are all talking about me. They are all talking behind my back.'

I bind the spirit of pride. I tell you right now you're not that important. Now if that offends you that is foolishness. Sometimes you have to have a sense of humour and get over yourself.

John Bevere calls the spirit of offense the bait of Satan. Why? Because he always has it out there for us. He is always trying to bait us into a place where we will be offended. If he can get me offended, he can rob me of my blessing. If he can get me under the spirit of offense he can open the door to conflict and strife, division, discord and disharmony. If he can get me offended, then he brings disunity to me and to the people in my life. I say to you, if there is conflict and strife in your life, then there is probably a spirit of offense that is behind it.

If you're thinking 'everyone is talking about me, someone is following me, everyone is against me, I am all alone in the world, you don't know what I have been through,' then you may have a spirit of offense on you and you need to deal with that or you are going to be robbed of your blessing.

If you find yourself gravitating to people all the time who are disgruntled, or in a place of disharmony, it is probably a familiar spirit of offense that continues to draw you to them.

Most of the time divorce comes from a spirit of offense. Betrayal opens the door, then disunity and disharmony and ultimately divorce.

If you are constantly going from relationship to relationship, from church to church, "heads up," it is probably not all the church's fault. If I am open to being offended, somebody is always going to offend me. If I allow myself to be offended, I will be.

I have to make a choice and a decision. The same way I made a choice never to drink again, I make a choice not to be offended, no matter what anybody says or does.

The spirit of Absalom is rooted in the spirit of offense. Absalom was the son of David. When his half brother raped his sister, he went and took revenge. He had a third party offense. He went and took revenge and then he got offended when his father took away his rights and cast him out of the Kingdom.

Finally, he was trying to talk to David's leader and he wouldn't come and talk to him, so Absalom lit his field on fire. He was pretty offended to do that. Then his dad lets him back in, but not all the way in. Absalom set himself up at the gate of the city and every time that David had to pass a judgment or make a ruling that went against someone, there was Absalom. Every time Absalom found someone who was offended, he drew them to him. Why did he thrive on offense? Because he was offended.

There could be 150 in a room and if two people have the spirit of offense they will find each other. If you constantly find yourself with someone who is offended there is a spirit of Absalom and a spirit of offense trying to draw you in.

THIRD PARTY OFFENSE

Here is a good example. A husband and wife get in a fight and you get in between them. The wife has been your friend for a long time and all of a sudden you are offended for her. Now the wife and husband make up and go on a vacation. Now they are away having a wonderful time and have forgiven each other but you are still back there suffering from a third party offense wondering how could she ever have gone away on a vacation with him.

Let's pray. Dear heavenly Father, I come to you in the name of Jesus Christ and in the power of the Holy Spirit. I bind the strong man of offence and every spirit related to the spirit of offence. I command you to loose your hold now of my brother/sister and leave now and go to the place that Jesus says to go, in Jesus' name. Father, I thank you right now for releasing a fresh anointing for deliverance and inner- healing into their lives and a fresh stirring of all the gifts and power of the Holy Spirit, Amen.

CHAPTER 9

TESTIMONIES

I want to share with you a few present day testimonies of Freedom Ministry. We have many wonderful testimonies of the power of God in deliverance and inner healing. I'd like to share a few, changing the names of course, to preserve the privacy of the people involved.

When I first came to Canada we did personal ministry right at the altar during the ministry time, and on a weekly basis, men and women would seek us out at home to minister to them. Many of these were Christian leaders who belonged to churches or denominations that didn't believe in this style of ministry. However, they were being harassed and tormented by demonic spirits. I was only in the country a few days and met up with Joan Gieson and her team for a healing conference in Brantford, Ontario. I prophesied that her ministry was going to a new spiritual level and that demonic spirits would begin to manifest and people were going to be set free by the power of God. At the first meeting we did together, toward the end of the service we are praying at two different sides of the altar and I heard her call out to me, "Honey, honey. . . ." When I got there a young lady was on the floor manifesting and thrashing around. I began to bind up spirits of rebellion and homosexuality and lesbianism and cast them out. After about twenty minutes of ministry she got up like a new person set free of many spirits. Glory to God! At a church in Brantford, we held a weekend workshop along with one of the pioneering couples in freedom ministry in Canada, Lovell and Isla McGuire. During that time, around January and February of 2001, many people were set free. A young female athlete about seventeen years old came to the workshop and the Lord set her free from many spirits that had troubled her and her family for many generations.

During the ministry time, Mave was trying to hold on to her because of the violent manifestations she was experiencing. When we were through, we looked at Mave's shoes and the leather was worn right off the tips. This young lady is still free today and beautifully serving the Lord in ministry.

We began to arrange personal private ministry sessions where many people set appointments to come in for more extensive ministry and I began to train and raise up teams to provide ministry to others and many of them are still involved with Eagle Worldwide today in ministry. I took them through and taught them at first to assist me then to do it themselves and raise up others as well. A man named Vincent Nero came to a men's conference to assist me and during the conference I began to bind up spirits and cast them out corporately. So many men were manifesting; I pressed Vincent into service he'd seen me do before but had never done on his own. That night he ministered freedom to eight or ten men to the Glory of God. He headed the men's team for me for many years and Pastored a Gypsy-Roma church for Eagle Worldwide in Toronto with his wife Mary. He also started a full gospel businessmen group and now serves together with his wife as pastors at Ignite Burlington, our One New Man work in that city.

In 2001, our traveling team was ministering at a wonderful church in Flamborough, Ontario. During the altar ministry time a gentleman came for prayer. He was shaking and one of the ladies on our team began to bind up spirits and cast them out and the shaking completely stopped. We went from there to Vineland, New Jersey and a woman came up with a huge goiter (a swelling in the thyroid gland) on her neck. Mave began to rebuke the generational spirits and the goiter kept going down right before our eyes.

Our team was on a mission trip to Trinidad and we were at Pastor Arnold's church, "We Care Fellowship" in San Fernando. During one of the nights, a seriously ill woman came to the service right from the hospital. She had been given no hope by the medical professionals. While being assisted back to her seat after the offering, she collapsed and people came to her aid including a person in the medical field, and found that she had no vital signs. Pastor Arnold's wife Sandra and Pastor Victoria Irving of EWWM and the Gathering Place church of Aurora began to bind up and cast out the spirits of death, illness, disease etc., and released words of life and hope and she was revived! Two years later on a return trip, this same woman came up to us. You could hardly recognize her, as she was vibrant and healthy. We had the privilege to interview her on video — what an amazing testimony of the power and love of God.

In September of 2000, I was ministering in a church in Pottstown, Pennsylvania. We were having such impactful meetings that they were extended for four weeks with services almost every night. One night around 11:00 p.m. and during the altar prayer time, I saw a man come into the church; he looked wild-eyed and was coming right towards me as I was praying in the front. He didn't really look friendly or appear that he was interested in prayer. When he got fairly close I lifted my hand in prayer toward him and he went right down on the ground with no catcher. I continued what I had been doing and came back his way again in a few minutes and he was just getting up again. I lifted my hand and asked the Lord to bless him and down he went again. I prayed some more and came back by him again and the same thing occurred. Then when I came back the next time he was sitting on the altar rail looking a little worn out but relatively normal and stone-cold sober. Later, Dave and his wife explained to me that he had been with his friends at a Flyers game and when he came home, his wife wasn't there and he was drunk and very upset knowing that she had been coming to the Holy Ghost meeting every night at this church. So he was coming to get her and straighten this thing out once and for all. He had a problem with alcohol, anger and other addictions and the Lord set him gloriously free that night. He began coming to the meetings and today more than eleven years later, he moved to Florida. He is still free married to the same wonderful wife and an Elder and leader in his church.

In 1999 I accompanied Pastor Wetzel to a church in Alabama. The first night we got there the worship team asked if I could go in and pray with them before the service. I asked Pastor Wetzel if he wouldn't mind me praying for them and got his permission to do so. They had a large and very talented team. We all gathered around in a circle and I began to pray. I started to bind up spirits of manipulation and control and witchcraft spirits and a Spirit of Jezebel and almost everyone in the room was manifesting all kinds of stuff. It was now 6:55 p.m. and the service was supposed to start in five minutes. I kept praying as hard as I could but it seemed to be getting worse and I didn't know what to do. Now, my Pastor is a wonderful man of God, but he is a bit particular about starting on time. I just didn't know what to do so I just opened the door and walked out and sat on the platform a couple seats away from Pastor. Some time passes and it's almost ten after seven and still no worship team. Pastor looks over at me and says, "Hey brother, what happened to the worship team?" I said, "Pastor, you're not going to believe this." He said, "Make me a believer." Just then, the worship team came out, they weren't looking too good and they began to worship and only did a couple of songs and turned it over to Pastor. He got up, looked over at me and didn't seem to be happy about the whole deal. Well, that night, thank you Jesus, the Lord began to move and Pastor couldn't even finish his message. We went out and began to pray for the people. It all ended well and Pastor forgot all about it. The next night when the worship team came out, the worship leader who was the pastor's wife, started off with a couple of beautiful songs then began to give her testimony about what happened the night before.

She said that some brother came in and prayed for our team and bound up Jezebel spirits and I got set totally free. She been operating in that spirit behind the scenes for a long time and was now free. The Spirit of the Lord began to move again and we went right to prayer and many people were set free of all kinds of spirits that night. Praise the Lord.

I brought a team to minister in Rochester, New York in 2001. We had an outreach on Ontario beach on the 4th of July with an outdoor bandstand and ministry tents. Many people were saved including some bikers. I had some young people with me and we served at the Rochester urban center where we fed quite a few homeless people and then went down under the city to the old abandon city where the homeless live bringing them food and clothes. On Sunday, we ministered at a local sponsoring church in the city. During the service I got a word of knowledge about someone's shoulder and the soundman came out of the booth as he was walking down the aisle. I saw a spirit in his shoulder and bound it up he crashed to the floor and I began to cast out the spirits for about five minutes and he was set free and returned to the booth. I had an altar call and a lot of people came forward and our team ministered deliverance to many. An older lady with a walker came up and she was pretty bent up with arthritis. As I bound the spirits she began to speak in a man's voice and attack me. I kept speaking and casting them out and moving backwards to get away until the Lord set her free and she walked out on her own with no walker. The next night the man in the sound booth looked like a new man and asked if he could give his testimony. He was the assistant pastor of the church and testified that he was under the influence of a spirit of pride; religious pride for many years and that the Lord had set him free the day before.

I could go on and on. Every week at the Kingsway Outreach Centre in downtown Hamilton, ON men and woman get saved, delivered, healed and set free by the power of God. At the Kingsway, we feed and serve nearly 200 people a day and many of those who now volunteer at the centre were part of the homeless and underprivileged community we serve, and were guests at the centre at one time. Three of them have graduated from our bible school, Spirit Ministries Training Centre, and our students go there every week and minister the power and love of the Gospel of Jesus Christ in a hands-on practical way.

Six of the churches we've planted have personal ministry teams set up doing deliverance and healing to individuals not only in our churches but to others in their community. Everyone on our traveling team and prayer teams gets personal ministry themselves before being released to travel with the team and then are trained how to facilitate it to others on a corporate and individual basis.

Our team has traveled to over 175 churches in North America, Europe, South America and the Caribbean in the last eleven years. The Holy Spirit did it in the ministry of Jesus Christ on earth in the lives of the early believers and apostles. He did it in the life of Paul who was born out of season, and the present day ministry of Christ though His disciples today. He is the same yesterday today and forever.

He wants to do it though you. Let's pray together. Heavenly Father, I thank you for the anointing to set the captive free and to bind up the broken hearted. I thank You for a release of the gifts and the power of the Holy Spirit into the lives of everyone reading this book. That they would receive a holy boldness to declare Your Word, to take authority over demonic spirits and demonstrate Your will and extend your kingdom on earth. I thank You Father that You are going to raise up warriors and anoint them to destroy the works of the devil in our generation. In Jesus' name. Amen.

CHAPTER 10

IN CONCLUSION

I'd like to leave you with a couple of thoughts. As I mentioned at the outset, this book was not meant to be a theological study but rather a journey of personal ministry experience. Many of you reading a book like 'Razing Hell,' on a subject like spiritual warfare, is in and of itself a stretch. If at all possible, if you are called to freedom ministry, attend some practical ministry workshops or enter an intern or apprentice program. Get some personal ministry yourself. If you feel called to freedom ministry or intercession or spiritual warfare, I urge you to align yourself properly with experienced professionals in the Body of Christ such as The International Society Of Deliverance Ministers. Get yourself some solid teaching and up to date information on the subject. Be sure you have proper spiritual covering and are approved and released to minister by your Pastor.

The ministry of deliverance and inner healing is personal in nature and requires you to minister from a place of compassion and confidentially. A solid personal discipleship walk is also very important along with adequate intercessory prayer covering. We, at Eagle Worldwide, hold a freedom workshop every summer during our summer camp meetings in Hamilton, Ontario.

This style of ministry is hand-to-hand combat so you want to take everything you do seriously. A walk of Holiness with no open doors in your life is important.

I want to pray with you. Heavenly Father, I come to You in the Name that is above every other Name, in the name of Jesus Christ and in the power of the Holy Spirit. I thank You for the anointing; I could never say thank You enough for the anointing, it's the anointing that destroys the yoke. I thank You for the power of impartation. I thank You for a release right now to my brother/sister of the anointing for deliverance, the anointing to set the captive free; for an impartation of the revelatory gifts, word of knowledge, word of wisdom and discerning of spirits. Let Your hand of blessing and Your hand of favor rest upon them. Place a hedge of protection around them. Place warrior angels around them and their families, homes, property and everything that is near and dear to them, and keep them safe, in Jesus Name, Amen.

Bibliography

Anderson, Dr. Neil T. Steps to Freedom in Christ. LaHabra, CA. 1993

Hammond, Frank and Ida Mae. Pigs in The Parlor – A Practical Guide to Deliverance. Kirkwood, Mo.: Impact Books, Inc., 1973.

Merck, Bobbie Jean. Spoiling Python's Schemes. Toccoa, Ga.: A Great, In.(c) 1990.

Moody, Gene and Earline. How to do Deliverance Manual. Baton Rouge, LA.

Worley, Win. Annihilating the Hosts of Hell – The Battle Royal – Book 1. Lansing II: HBC Publications, (c) 1891.

Worley, Win. Conquering the Hosts of Hell – Diary of an Exorcist. Lansing II: HBC Publications, (c) 1980.

Worley, Win. Conquering the Hosts of Hell – An Open Triumph. Lansing II: HBC Publications, (c) 1983.

Worley, Win. Demolishing the Hosts of Hell – Every Christian's Job. Lansing, II: HBC Publications, (c) 1983.

William Sudduth, So Free – Chosen Books, a division of Baker Publishing Group, 2003.

William Sudduth, Behind the Ink – Chosen Books, a division of Baker Publishing Group, 2004.

**Special Recognition: A large portion of this material was provided by Roger and Donna Miller of Trumpet of Gideon

Ministries, 2019 Cedarmount Drive, Franklin, Tennessee 37067; from their "Manual for Deliverance Workers."

** Special Recognition as well to Bill and Janet Sudduth of Colorado Springs, Colorado who provided us with a number of special prayers, particularly those having to do with occult groups and Free Masons and their descendants. Bill is President of The International Society of Deliverance Ministries and a powerful teacher of deliverance and inner healing.

Russ Moyer

Russ Moyer is presently a missionary/evangelist in Ontario, Canada. He is the founder and president of Eagle Worldwide Ministries. Since his arrival in Canada in October of 2000, he has established the Eagle Traveling Team, which has visited more than 80 churches in North America, Europe, and the Caribbean. He also founded the Eagle Worldwide Retreat and Revival Centre, a beautiful 50+ acre parcel of ground in Copetown, Ontario where annually Summer Camp Tent meetings July through Labour Day along with special conferences and events such as Parade of the Nations, School of the Prophets, and The Elisha Leadership Mentoring Intern Program for youth and young adults.

Russ and his wife Mave have pioneered eight churches in southern Ontario, and are the senior pastors of both The Revival Centre in Hamilton and Eagles' Nest Fellowship in Ancaster. They also provide spiritual covering and apostolic oversight for eight other churches and more than 60 ministers through the Eagle Worldwide Network of Ministries. In May of 2005, John Kelly, C. Peter Wagner and the International Coalition of Apostles commissioned Russ in his apostolic calling and office.

Russ and Mave have a heart to see revival in people groups all over the earth. The Lord continues to open doors for them to minister to indigenous people groups such as the Inuit in the Arctic, the First Nations people in Hawaii, here in Ontario, and in Saskatchewan. In January of 2009 they birthed a First Nations church on the Six Nations Reserve in Ontario. They have also ministered extensively to Africans, Portuguese, French, and the Gypsy Roma peoples.

They are also the founders of Eagle Worldwide Foundation, and The Centre for Excellence, which provides empowerment, educational, and training programs for the underprivileged. This project includes the founding of The King's Way Blessing Centre where they feed and service over 250 clients per day free of charge in the inner city of Hamilton.

Russ and Mave also birthed Spirit Ministries Training Centre, a 2-year practical ministry Bible school.

Russ was a successful businessman for over 21 years and was the recipient of many honors in the business community. He was the founder, president, and CEO of a number of security related businesses, and at one time employed more than two hundred people. He also was the executive producer and host of a weekly, one-hour television program, which dealt with some of the serious issues facing American families, emphasizing Christian values.

In 1997 he traveled to Pensacola, Florida to attend the Brownsville Revival School of Ministry. He graduated in December 1999 and was ordained by Ruth Ward Heflin through Calvary Pentecostal Tabernacle in Ashland, Virginia. Brother Russ is used heavily in the prophetic, deliverance, and healing ministries. He has a heart to see revival in Canada and the nations.

Mave Moyer

Reverend Mave Moyer is an ordained minister, and she ministers alongside her husband Brother Russ Moyer. They both currently pastor The Revival Centre in Hamilton and Eagles' Nest Fellowship in Copetown, Ontario. They also serve as the apostolic overseers for eight other church plants in Ontario as well as the Eagle Worldwide Retreat and Revival Centre. Mave is the governing official for the Eagle Worldwide Network of Ministries, a spiritual covering for licensed Christian Workers, ministers, churches, missionaries, and para-church organizations.

Pastor Mave is an anointed teacher and preacher in her own right, with a heart to deliver a "Now word" to the Body of Christ. She moves powerfully in the gift of faith, healing, and the prophetic. She is also a gifted singer and poetic psalmist who brings forth "the song of the Lord." She has been involved in producing many country/comedy shows, Christian dinner theatre, and Inner Circle Gospel sings.

She has had the privilege to work and travel with Joan Gieson, a healing evangelist who founded Ministries of Love out of St. Louis, Missouri. Mave attended Rhema Bible Training Centre in Tulsa, Oklahoma.

Eagle Worldwide Ministries

Eagle Worldwide Ministries is a prophetic ministry called to bring revival fire to the nations and to challenge, empower and equip the church of Jesus Christ with a powerful message of holiness and hope.

We will focus on the restoration of foundational truths, preparing and equipping the saints for the end-time harvest through teaching, impartation and demonstrations of the gifts of the Holy Spirit.

Eagle Worldwide Ministries includes:

- Seven churches in Ontario that were birthed through dreams and revelations and one in Buffalo, NY:
    - The Gathering Place, Aurora, ON
    - Eagle's Nest Fellowship, Copetown, ON
    - Caleb's Place, Orillia, ON
    - The Revival Centre, Hamilton, ON
    - Eagles' Nest Six Nations, Ohsweken, ON
    - Ignite Burlington, Burlington, ON
    - His Glory House, Toronto, ON
    - Eagles' Nest Buffalo/Niagara, Elma, NY

- The Retreat and Revival Centre, a place where believers can come and be trained, equipped, and prepared for Christian service.
- Eagle Worldwide Network of Ministries, which is an apostolic and prophetic network that provides spiritual covering, credentialing, and fellowship to churches, ministries, missionaries, Christian businesspeople and government workers that are pursuing their call in church or in the marketplace.

**Eagle Worldwide Ministries
Retreat and Revival Centre**

Summer Camp Meetings
Come and Get in the Glory!

Second week of July through Labour Day Weekend
Every night at 7:00 p.m.

Every year we hold ten weeks of summer camp at our 50+ acre Retreat Centre. We begin the season with our Parade of Nations, and hold other events and functions, as well as performing water baptisms right in our beautiful lakes!

Spring Camp Meetings

Every year we also host Spring Camp, a 10-day conference in April with anointed Apostolic and Prophetic ministers. We hold special week long courses in conjunction with our Bible School, Spirit Ministries Training Centre that can be taken for audit or credit in our Bible School. For more information, visit us at: www.SpiritMinistries.ca

For more information contact us at:

P.O. Box 39
Copetown, ON, L0R 1J0, CANADA
Tel.: (905) 308-9991
Fax: (905) 308-7798
http://www.EagleWorldwide.com
office@eagleworldwide.com
Ministry DVDs and CDs available from every service.

Eagle Worldwide Network of Ministries

Dr. Russ and Pastor Mave Moyer are the Apostolic overseers of the Eagle Worldwide Network of Ministries, which is a company of apostolic leaders, churches and ministries committed to walk in a covenant relationship with Eagle Worldwide Ministries based on a common vision of a fully functioning New Testament Church.

Our vision is to build a network of churches, ministries and leaders committed to train and release believers in their care into their call and ministry. We believe that all the gifts of the Spirit in the New Testament are for today and that every ministry in the New Testament including prophecy and deliverance is for today. We also believe that there is no junior Holy Spirit and that both youth and children can and should be equipped and released in ministry. We proceed on the basis that the release of the gifts of the Holy Spirit is not to be restricted by age, race, gender or class. This group will come from varied backgrounds including Christian businessmen and women.

Presently we provide spiritual covering and credentialing for more than one hundred ministers, ministries, and churches in North America.

For more information on our Network of Ministries call us during regular business hours at (905) 308-9991 or email us at: network@eagleworldwide.com. You can also visit the Network section of our website at:

www.EagleWorldwide.com

ELISHA PROJECT
Online Mentoring

Mave and I have traveled extensively across North America and other parts of the world. Almost everywhere we go people talk to us about discipleship and mentoring because that is really our heart and at the heart of Eagle Worldwide Ministries. I believe that is the prophetic season we are in as well from Malachi 4, the hearts of the children being turned back to the fathers and the hearts of the fathers being turned back to the children. I believe we all realize that in the natural we have experienced a fatherless generation. Unfortunately, it's been like that as well in the church. And many people suffer because they were never properly discipled and mentored.

The Elisha Project is all about raising up this next generation: preparing, empowering and equipping them, launching them into their harvest. These are the days of Elijah; these are the days of the harvest. The fields are white and ready for harvest. It's time for the Elijah's and the Elisha's to walk together, to work together.

For more information on the Elisha Project visit:

www.AriseGlory.com

<u>Mentoring courses available</u>

Foundations   Leadership/Mentoring   Dreams & Visions
Prophetic Mentoring   Church Government/Birthing/Building
Deliverance/Freedom Streams   Marketplace Ministry

Resources

Night Watch: Unlocking Your Destiny Through Dreams and Visions

Can These Bones Live?: Restoring the Church

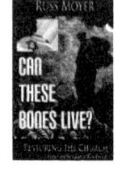

Living on the Prophetic Edge

Leading on the Prophetic Edge

Teaching CD's, Ministry DVD's, books, manuals, prophetic series and more can be found by visiting our online bookstore.

The Prophetic Edge is a newsletter written by Dr. Russ Moyer to help you as you seek the Lord in pursuing you're prophetic gifting and calling.

To receive The Prophetic Edge, visit our website and register your name and we will email it to you every month for free.

Internet

http://www.EagleWorldwide.com
Eagle Worldwide Ministry Website

http://www.IntegritySingles.com
A singles community with a focus on Integrity

http://www.AriseGlory.com
A Christian Network Resourcing and Referral Centre

http://www.SpiritMinistries.ca
A practical, hands on Spirit led Bible School

http://www.facebook.com/eagleworldwide
Facebook

http://twitter.com/#!BroRussMoyer
Twitter

http://wwwlinkedin.com
Linked In

If you are interested in having your Christian book published through Eagle Worldwide Publication call us. Services we offer:

- Review and proofread your manuscript
- Format your book to your specifications
- Cover design. We can offer you as much or as little help in the publication process as you need. For more information please contact us at:

Tel.: (905) 308-9991
Fax: (905) 308-7798
E-mail: office@eagleworldwide.com

For we do not wrestle against flesh and blood, but against principalities, against powers, against the rulers of the darkness of this age, against spiritual hosts of wickedness in the heavenly places.

**Ephesians 6:12
SPIRIT OF STRIFE**

*For where envy and strife exist, confusion
and every evil will be there.*

James 3:16

Helmet of Pride	Hammer of Judgment
Breastplate of Unrighteousness	Cloak of Deception
Sword of Bitterness	Boots of Anger
Shield of Hate	Speaking Forth Lies